EGYPTIAN
MYTHOLOGY

EGYPTIAN MYTHOLOGY

PAUL HAMLYN · LONDON

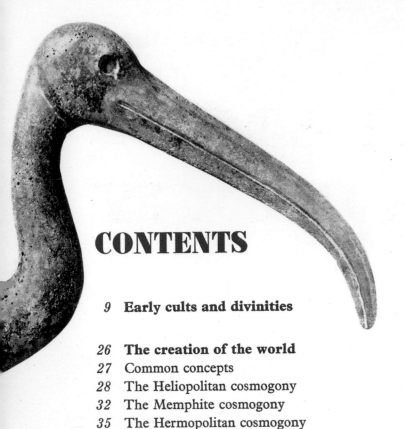

CONTENTS

Paul Hamlyn Limited
Drury House, Russell Street, London, WC2
First Edition Jan. 1965
Second Impression 1965
Third Impression 1966
© 1965 Paul Hamlyn Limited
Printed in Czechoslovakia by Svoboda, Prague

Egyptian Mythology
based on the text translated by
Delano Ames from Mythologie Générale
Larousse
first published by
Augé, Gillon, Hollier-Larousse,
Moreau & Cie

COLOUR PLATES

Acknowledgments

The Publishers gratefully acknowledge the following for permission to reproduce the illustrations indicated:

Colour Plates:

British Museum: *21, 116, 117, 135.* Forman Bros: *Back cover, 77.* Giraudon: *1, 39.* A. F. Kersting: *20.* Shell Photographic Unit: *22.* Scala Instituto Fotografico: *115.* Roger Wood: *Front cover, 2, 19, 40, 41, 42, 59, 60, 78, 95, 96, 97, 98, 118, 136.*

Black and white illustrations

Alinari: *10—11, 17, 23, 54, 61, 70, 80, 90 (top), 91, 106, 113, 141 (bottom).* Archiv für Kunst und Geschichte: *13 (both pictures), 66, 88 (left), 127, 141 (top).* Archives Photographiques: *28 (both pictures), 149.* Audrain-Samivel: *16.* Bavaria-Verlag: *74, 76, 92, 125 (bottom),* Boucher: *142.* British Museum: *14, 26—27, 30—31 (both pictures), 35, 47 (right), 48 (left), 52, 63, 74, 83 (right), 93, 105, 128 (both pictures), 129, 130, 131, 133, 143 (both pictures), 145, 147, 148.* Bulloz: *24 (left), 34, 112, 120, 131, 138, 140, 146.* Cairo Museum: *12.* Fitzwilliam Museum, Cambridge: *7.* Forman Bros: front and back endpapers *8, 29, 33, 68—69, 75, 99, 107, 121.* Giraudon: *69, 94 (left).* A. F. Kersting: *67.* Larousse: *11, 53.* Mansell Collection: *36, 47 (left), 48 (right), 49, 56, 72, 79, 81 (top), 88 (right), 100, 101, 103, 104, 119, 122 (left), 126, 130, 144.* Oropeza: *64.* Photo Marburg: *15, 18, 24 (right), 38, 55, 65, 81 (bottom), 83 (left), 90 (bottom), 102, 108—109, 110.* Paul Popper: *51, 89.* Radio Times Hulton Picture Library: *58, 123.* Shell Photographic Unit: *25, 122 (right), 132.* Roger Viollet: *9, 32, 37, 43, 44, 57, 84, 86—87, 94 (right), 124, 125 (bottom), 139.*

EARLY CULTS AND DIVINITIES

No one who strolls through the Egyptian galleries of a museum can fail to be struck by the multitude of divinities attracting attention on all sides. Colossal statues in sandstone, granite and basalt, minute statuettes in glazed composition, bronze or gold, portray gods and goddesses frozen in hieratic or symbolical attitudes, seated or standing. Sometimes these male or female figures have heads with human features. More often they have the head of an animal, or a human head surmounted by an animal symbol such as a falcon, a jackal, a scarab beetle. As we shall see later, these animal symbols serve to indicate not only the particular god being represented but also the especial aspect of his character or legend that is being emphasised. Artistic representation thus becomes of more than usually great interest in the study of the myths. It was important to the Egyptian believer that his religious monuments should be built of lasting material. As a result a great wealth of artistic evidence has been preserved. The well-known pyramids and temples on the ancient sites are not only monuments to the enormous secular power of the rulers of Egypt, they are also in themselves symbolic of some of the religious beliefs which we shall be discussing. The treasures in them and those which have been removed to our museums often include more direct reference to the myths. The divinities that figure in these myths can be seen again and again receiving adoration and offerings or performing ritual gestures for the benefit of their worshippers on the bas-reliefs of massive sarcophagi or sculpted on funerary stelae and stone blocks stripped from temple walls. They recur on mummy cases and in the pictures which illuminate papyri, or manuscripts.

In view of such a multiplicity of divine images it may seem strange to suggest that the religion of ancient Egypt is very imperfectly known to us. Such, however, is the case; though we know the names of these gods and goddesses and the temples in which they were worshipped, we understand little of their nature and seldom know even the legends concerning them. Only slowly are scholars beginning to learn more about the nature of Egyptian religion. The artistic representations of religious subjects are in general more concerned with the cult or ritual than with the depiction of mythological stories. Herein lies the clue to much of our difficulty in understanding the Egyptian religion, and indeed our difficulty in understanding much primitive belief. Unlike modern man, the ancient Egyptian seems not to have felt the need of logic or consistency in his religion. Though all-embracing and dominating every aspect of the individual's life, his religion was not fixed and static in a dogmatic creed; it was rather a creative religion, where every believer was called on to use his imagination. Each enactment of ritual was not only a reminder of some legend concerned with the gods, it also *was* those events. On the other hand, any deviation from the accustomed ritual, for whatever reason, could entail a revision of the original legend. This, apart from the many centuries with their differing conditions during which the Egyptian religion prevailed, may account for the variations and inconsistencies which are apparent between the various sources of our

The Fourth-Dynasty pyramid of Khephren at Giza, almost 450 feet high and made of limestone from the cliffs lining the Nile Valley. Elaborate tombs of the pharaohs, the pyramids were built partly by slave labour and partly by agricultural workers in the season of the Nile's floods.

9

Left: *Woman worshipping the goddess Hathor.*

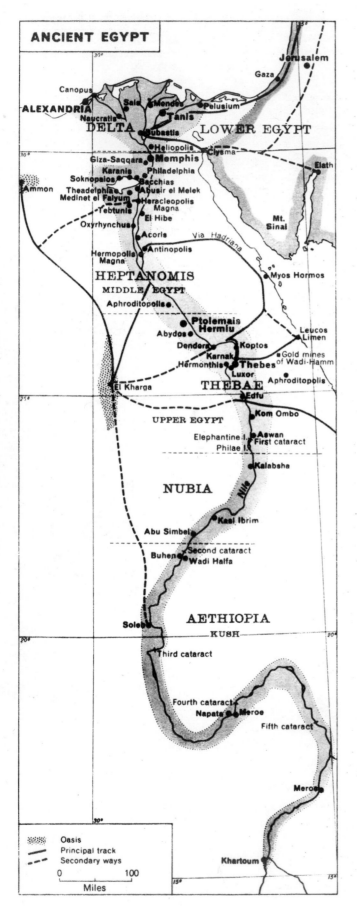

ANCIENT EGYPT

Jerusalem
Gaza
Canopus
ALEXANDRIA
Sais · Mendes · Pelusium
Naucratis · Tanis
DELTA · Bubastis LOWER EGYPT
· Heliopolis Clysma
Giza-Saqqara · Memphis
Karanis · Philadelphia Elath
Soknopaios · Bacchias
Theadelphia · Abusir el Melek
Medinet el Faiyum
· Tebtunis Heracleopolis
Magna
· El Hibe
Oxyrhynchus Mt.
Sinai
Ammon
Acoris
Via Hadriana
· Antinopolis
Hermopolis
Magna Myos Hormos
HEPTANOMIS
MIDDLE EGYPT
Aphroditopolis
Ptolemais
Hermiu Leucos
Abydos Limen
Dendera Koptos
Karnak · Gold mines
Hermonthis Thebes of Wadi-Hamm
Luxor
Aphroditopolis
El Kharga THEBAE
· Edfu
Kom Ombo
UPPER EGYPT
Elephantine I. · Aswan
Philae I. First cataract
· Kalabsha
NUBIA
Kasr Ibrim
Abu Simbel
Second cataract
Buhen Wadi Halfa
AETHIOPIA
Soleb KUSH
Third cataract
Fourth cataract
Napata · Meroe
Fifth cataract
Meroe
Khartoum

Oasis
Principal track
Secondary ways
0   100
Miles

This stela (an inscribed memorial stone commemorating the dead) reflects the importance of the pyramid in Egyptian ritual. Eighteenth Dynasty.

Left: *The concentration of its cities along the narrow strip of the cultivable river valley emphasises ancient Egypt's dependence on the Nile. Without its waters no community could have existed.*

knowledge of the religion. There is some reason to believe that the Egyptians might have regarded what we would term inconsistencies as something like the differences between two poems interpreting the same theme; each had its own justification in the imagination of its author. In general, too, and certainly in the later periods, the Egyptians seem to have consciously regarded their gods as symbols — no more — of cosmic or ethical forces. Modern scholars increasingly reject the view, for instance, that the Egyptians worshipped animals themselves as gods; rather they worshipped the qualities which they conceived these animals to be endowed with.

Just as the Egyptians made little distinction between cult and theology, so the boundaries between religion and what we should nowadays call politics were ill-defined. In so far as 'Church'

Right: *The Hyksos sphinx at Tanis is a reminder of Egypt's long occupation by its earliest invaders. The sphinx, with the body of a lion and the head of a man, a hawk or a ram, symbolised the union of physical and intellectual power.*

and 'State' can be distinguished in ancient Egypt it is clear that each supported the other. The king was regarded as divine and his rule on earth amounted to a ritual re-enactment of mythological events. A large part of mythology such as we know it is concerned therefore with the setting up of a hierarchy on earth, with a system of land tenure and with the establishment of ritual forms. Egyptian mythology can therefore be interpreted as an attempt to bolster up the authority of the king, and certainly some changes in religious belief can be traced to the opening of a new dynasty or a shift of power from one part of the country to another. This, however, though an interesting aspect, is an essentially modern view of the situation. The ancient Egyptian really believed that his king had divine authority, not merely that he claimed it as a justification for his rule. He believed that the

king was the direct intermediary between the gods and men, and that without the king the divine benefits could not extend to the ordinary inhabitants of the country. The king's actions and his welfare were therefore of prime importance to every one of his subjects. As we shall see, the welfare of the pharaoh's soul after death was of equal if not of greater importance. To this fact we owe the most complete literature we have on the Egyptian religion. The funerary service known as *The Book of the Dead*, whose purpose was to ensure the safe passage of the pharaohs to the after world, gives us the best clues to the legends alluded to in the mythological scenes of art. Though innumerable religious texts have survived which contain references to mythological occurrences, the full stories are almost never set down; for they were known to every early Egyptian and handed down

11

from generation to generation by word of mouth alone. Such, at least, is our belief, for full-length stories from the myths have survived only from a fairly late period.

The Egyptian mythological texts are the oldest known religious literature, the earliest texts dating from about the middle of the third millennium B.C. This in itself tells us something about the land in which it arose. Just as in modern Egypt the Nile and the sun together impart fertility and a regular pattern to life on the Nile's banks, making it rich agricultural land, so in ancient times the river imposed an agricultural pattern and the intense sun promoted the growth of crops. Egypt was a natural geographical unit, and it very early became a political unit as well. There was a reverse side to the benefits conferred by the Nile and by the sun: the Nile floods could, and often did, fail; the sun was visibly a destructive as well as a creative force. The surrounding desert, which gave Egypt physical unity was also a constant reminder to the valley inhabitants of their special dependence on the beneficent influence of Nature. All primitive peoples seek in some way to understand the world in which they live. The violent contrasts of the Nile valley may have stimulated the Egyptians more than most to enquire into the nature of their surroundings.

At the beginning, certainly, each tribe must have had its own god — one suited to the life of that particular group. Thus different cults became localised in specific areas of the Nile valley, and differing religious systems grew up about the various cult centres. Our knowledge of these comes from what appear to be the earliest representations of Egyptian deities. They date from about the middle of the fourth millennium, long before the first hieroglyphs. The god of each tribe seems to have been incarnated in the form of an animal, of a bird or of a simple fetish. There is a fragment of a palette for grinding malachite in the Louvre on which we see men of one of these early tribes setting forth to hunt. They are bearded, unlike the clean-shaven men of later historical epochs, and they wear only a belted loin-cloth. The bushy tail of an animal is attached to the back of the belt. At the head of the group marches the tribal chief. In one hand he brandishes a club; in the other he grasps the staff of a standard or totem pole which bears a kind of perch for a falcon. In other examples of this type of scene the falcon is replaced

The victory palette of Narmer, the first king to rule the North and South. He is seen brandishing a mace over a captive. The Horus falcon, indicating his divinity, tramples underfoot plants symbolic of the Delta. First Dynasty. Cairo Museum.

Top right: *Roman bas-relief of a procession of the followers of Isis. Egyptian religion attracted adherents over a very long period, from the middle of the fourth millennium until the middle of the sixth century A.D., when the cult of Isis was still pursued in the island of Philae.*

Right: *A bronze statue of Bast, the benevolent cat-goddess of Bubastis. Animals and birds were widely worshipped in early Egypt — probably for the qualities they displayed. Frequently the cult was local, and often a creature held sacred in one city was regarded elsewhere as the enemy of mankind.*

by an elephant, a goat, an ibis, a jackal, a scorpion, or perhaps by a thunderbolt, or two crossed arrows on a shield.

As we shall see, these symbols were to retain their significance far into the historical period, for later cults incorporated them into their own systems. Records of the religion practised in Egypt extend over a longer span of time than those for any other religion — and though the cult underwent some changes, which we shall examine, basically the same religion obtained throughout all this period. If we accept that later accretions do not constitute an entirely new religion, then we must recognise that the Egyptian religion was in fact one with an unusually long life: its earliest manifestations date, as we have seen, from the middle of the fourth millennium, and it was not finally eradicated in its later forms until the middle of the sixth century A.D., when the cult of Isis was still carried on in the island of Philae. It was not only derivations and developments that survived to a relatively late date; indeed animal worship of the kind that we generally associate with the earlier ages was revived in the Graeco-Roman period in an attempt to counter the influence of foreign religions by emphasis on essentially Egyptian cults. In the same way and with the same intention the cult of

13

an aspect of a great god as a local deity was revived at the same period; universalising tendencies which had certainly been native to Egypt, but which foreign influence had intensified, led the priests to encourage a reversion to aspects of Egyptian religion which the official cults had superseded.

It is interesting to note that even in prehistoric times these animal symbols as gods of the tribe led their followers into battle and, when necessary, fought for them: from the earliest times, therefore, the chieftain has become identified with a god, for often one of the divine animal's paws is a human hand which grasps a weapon to slaughter an enemy or an implement to attack his fortress.

These animal deities, however, gradually gave way to gods in human form, and at the end of his anthropomorphic evolution nothing of the primitive animal is left except the head surmounting the body of a man or woman. Sometimes the head too has become human and all that remains are vestigial ears or horns.

From the Second Dynasty on — that is from the beginning of the third millennium — the divine types seem to be fixed as far as artistic representation is concerned. Thus art provides an element of continuity throughout three millennia, whatever the significance attributed to the gods at different periods may have been.

Like the hunters of the ancient tribes, the gods of the historical epoch are shown dressed in short loin-cloths ornamented by animals' tails. The goddesses, like great ladies, wear a narrow robe, held at the shoulders by shoulder-straps and falling nearly to their ankles. Though these gods and goddesses acquired new and more sophisticated attributes with the passage of time, they often retained the head of the animal from which they were derived. They wear heavy wigs, thanks to which the transition between the snout of an animal or the beak of a bird and their human bodies takes place so smoothly that our aesthetic sense is

Granite coffin lid of Meri-Mes, a governor of the Sudan. Eighteenth Dynasty. British Museum.

Right: *Head of Seti I from a relief in the temple at Abydos. The divinity of the pharaoh was accepted from very early times and he was regarded as the sun-god reigning on earth.*

scarcely troubled, and these hybrid beings seem almost real.

At other times the head is human, and in this case the shaven chin of the god is adorned with an artificial plaited beard, which recalls the beards of the first Egyptians.

These divinities are distinguished and immediately identified by their different head-dresses and by various attributes inherited from the original fetish or from the primitive animal which surmounts their heads. Sometimes, too, their names are written in the hieroglyphic signs. Like the ancient tribal chieftains, the gods carry sceptres with one end forked and the other decorated by, say, the head of a greyhound. Goddesses bear in their hand a simple stalk of papyrus.

By the time that the animals and fetishes of the prehistoric epoch had become divinities in human form the nomad warriors whom they once led into battle had long since settled down to till the soil. It seems that even when the early Egyptians were still primarily dependent on hunting for food, they had learnt that the physical conditions of the Nile valley could best be exploited by men grouped into settlements: the soil was fertile, but if it was to produce crops it had to be carefully irrigated. Organised communities developed early in order to meet this need, and social and political systems were inevitably connected with the forces of fertility and life. The gods of the hunting tribes were not abandoned by the agricultural descendants of their early worshippers. But as we shall observe time and time again in the course of Egyptian history, the gods, being a reflection not only of immutable spiritual needs, but also of the physical and, in modern terms, the political condition of a people, were adapted through the ages to conform with changing circumstances. The gods of the hunters retained part of their old character, and especially the symbols which denoted them in art and in ritual. This is an essential feature of the Egyptian religion, and one which modern man finds difficult to grasp. To our minds there seems to be a curious duality in the function of these beliefs: they reflected the contemporary established order, and at the same time they served to justify it. In this sense their function is similar to that of primitive magic, where the depiction of a situation

15

Horus, Osiris and Isis formed a triad worshipped particularly at Philae. The number three seems to have had a mystical significance for the Egyptians, and their principal gods were generally worshipped in a triad, the third member proceeding from the other two. Thus Horus is the child of Osiris and Isis and inferior to them in the triad.

Left: *A colonnade in the temple of Luxor, built during the reign of Amenhotep III. Eighteenth Dynasty.*

in ritual images, or still more strongly, the ritual declamation of it would make the events in question actually occur or would give a situation the force of law. This is an essential concept and will explain much of the agglomerative or syncretic tendencies of the Egyptian religion.

At first, each god was installed in the town built by one of the now settled tribes, and was thus transformed from a tribal into a local god. Every town, village and district had its god who bore the title 'Lord of the City'. There he resided and yielded priority of rank to no one. Conceived in the image of a man, but a man of infinite strength and power, he possessed a vital fluid — the *ka* — which he could renew at will by having another god, better endowed, lay hands on him. He delighted in revealing himself to men, and he would become incarnate in the temple statue, in a fetish, or in a chosen animal which the initiated could recognise by certain signs.

The god resided in the temple, which was his palace. Only pharaoh, the king, whom he called his 'son' had the right to appear in his presence. But as the king could naturally not officiate everywhere at once he delegated high priests to each sanctuary to perform in his place the ceremonies of the cult, while numerous priests and priestesses composed the domestic staff of the god and administered his sometimes immense domains. The priesthood therefore acquired great importance and power, and it became customary for it to be an hereditary office. The main function of the priestesses in the ritual seems to have been to dance and make music in the forecourt, but in some temples, such as that of Amon, where the god venerated was particularly noted for his fertility associations, the priestesses were deemed to be concubines of the god.

On certain dates the 'Lord of the City' brought joy to his people by deigning to show himself to them in all his glory. Abandoning the deep shadows of the *naos* (the inner sanctuary of the temple) where only pharaoh's representative had the privilege of worshipping him daily, he would emerge majestically and be borne through the streets in his golden barque on the shoulders of his priests. Such expeditions were partly considered to be a treat, a kind of annual outing, for the god; more importantly, they were in some cases the occasion for petitions direct to the god from some individual, and as the god advanced towards the petitioner

17

or retreated from him, his case was judged to be just or not. The god did not normally make such direct intervention in the lives of men. The extent to which he had been pleased by his people was shown only in their degree of prosperity. In general the god's needs were thought of as being similar to those of human beings, and the chief features of the daily ritual were the administration of an elaborate toilet to the god, who was anointed and decked with jewels, and the presentation of a meal.

In early times the god lived alone, jealous of his authority. But the Egyptian could not conceive of life without a family, and soon married off his god or goddess and gave him or her a son, thus forming a divine triad or trinity in which the father, moreover, was not always the chief, contenting himself with the role of prince consort, while the principal deity of the locality remained the goddess. This occurred, for example, at Dendera, where the sovereign was the goddess Hathor. In historical terms, such creation of families or hierarchies was often the outcome of the growth of political power of the city whose god was thus elevated at the expense of cities which worshipped the subordinate deities. By the end of the fourth millennium unification of such districts had advanced so far that only two great divisions remained: Upper Egypt and Lower Egypt. The early years of the third millennium saw the union of Upper and Lower Egypt, and from that point on the wealth and power of Egypt rapidly grew, and with it a rich cultural life.

From what has already been said, it will be clear that such unification will have led to far greater religious complexity rather than to the domination of one god to the exclusion of all others. The ancient Egyptians seem to have been essentially conservative in their outlook, and found it almost impossible to reject any previously held notions. On the other hand, they were exceptionally tolerant in their attitude to other beliefs than their own, and seem to have taken the view that whatever men believe in must have some validity, almost by virtue of their believing in it. They therefore found it easy to fall in with their rulers' natural desire that political union should be mirrored by religious union, just as all political events had their counterpart in the realm of mythology and ritual. The beliefs justified the cult, and the cult justified the temporal power.

It is therefore true to say that, by and large, during the period when Egypt was a unified country all the gods which had formerly been local divinities were worshipped throughout the land. Special prominence may have been given to a particular god in the city or region of that god's provenance, but he was in general related in some mythological scheme to the other gods worshipped in the remainder of Egypt. Though the Egyptians never seem to have attached much importance to creating a systematically and logically formulated mythological scheme or pantheon such as the Greeks or the Romans elaborated, certain great political changes involving a shift of power from one city to another were reflected in the mythological sphere by a shift in the relative importance of particular gods or of aspects of their cult. Basically, the most prominent of the gods throughout the history of ancient Egypt in some way represented the powers of creation or fertility. In the Nile valley such powers were readily identified with the sun, and the sun accordingly lent at least some of its attributes to whatever deity was currently the most prominent. Even the cult of Osiris, which dominated Egyptian religion in later times, was gradually changed from a cult of the dead to a cult of fertility or of life, even if this was life after death. As we shall see, Osiris became increasingly identified with the sun and gradually entered the realm of the living. The association of

Left: *The temple at Dendera, the cult centre of Hathor. Construction began in the first century B.C. and finished during the rule of Augustus in the first century A.D. Its walls bear scenes and inscriptions of the festivals associated with Hathor.*

The four deities of the sanctuary at Abu Simbel: Ptah, Amon-Ra, Rameses and Ra-Harakhte.

Top left: *The Step Pyramid at Sakkara.*
Bottom left: *Great Sphinx at Giza.*

Right: *Seker as a mummified falcon. From the Papyrus of Ani. British Museum.*

*Painting from the tomb of Horemheb (1384—
1328 B.C.) showing him on the left facing Osiris
and in the centre offering wine to Hathor, Queen
of the West.*

the cult of the dead with fertility cults was, of course, not unique to Egypt. It occurs again in the Greek myth of Hades and Persephone. This may be why the myth of Osiris particularly interested Plutarch when he visited Egypt. The Osiris myth cycle is one of the few that has been transmitted to us in any detail, and it is to Plutarch that we owe this. Though Greek and writing of times already long past, he was evidently well informed; for in ancient texts we find frequent references to the events he relates, notably in those texts which the old kings of the Sixth Dynasty had engraved inside their pyramids — twenty-five centuries before him. Even in the oldest myths, death is not unknown to the gods; in the times of the earliest settlements the 'Lord of the City' could not defend himself for ever against old age, and sometimes he even died.

The god Horus was in the beginning an exception to the general rule that the chief gods were associated with fertility or creation. He seems originally to have been one of the gods of the early tribes. Symbolised by a falcon, he was the hunters' god or possibly a war-god, for his tribe is thought to have imposed itself on its neighbours and perhaps to have achieved the unification of Upper Egypt. The falcon thus became the symbol of majesty and the archetype of the pharaohs. Later attempts to incorporate worship of the sun into the Horus legend took the form of making the divine falcon a sky-god, the sun being his right eye and the moon his left eye, or of making Horus the son of Ra. In later times this falcon-Horus was confused with another god called Horus who was the son of Isis and Osiris or the son of Geb and Nut and therefore the grandson of the sun-god. The composite god which emerged from this confusion retained the falcon symbol and the associations with majesty and power, but he also figured in the Underworld myths of Osiris. On the other hand, his association with the Osiris myth helps to explain how Osiris gradually left the realm of the dead and entered that of the living, and both gods have important roles in the interplay of myths and ritual concerning the living and the dead which increasingly dominated the Egyptian religion. It seems unlikely that Osiris and the cult of the dead or ancestor worship would have attained such importance if the two Horus gods had not been confused.

Funerary stela of a follower of Amon. In the upper panel the deceased appears before Osiris, the judge of the dead. In the lower panel, Hathor, with a cow's head, is seen giving the bread and water of life to the soul. Nineteenth Dynasty.

23

Though in this sense there is continuity or perhaps a cyclic pattern in the formulation of Egyptian beliefs, religious systems were by no means left to evolve naturally in the minds of the people at large. It would be wrong to over-emphasise the deliberate changing of doctrine by kings or by priests to suit their own ambitions, but it is impossible to understand such knowledge as we have of beliefs held about the various gods without some consideration of the basic systems of the great cult centres. Contemporary evidence of the beliefs of the Egyptians is contained in religious documents produced in these cult centres. These documents are couched in symbolic language referring to mythological events as understood in each centre. We are thus able to guess at the underlying systems by examining the implications of the ritual embodied in the texts. Before we discuss each individual god, it is necessary to consider the doctrines of the four great cult centres, Heliopolis, Hermopolis, Memphis and Thebes. The cult of Osiris, which gradually supplanted these systems, will be discussed separately.

The body of myths, many of which are common to the whole of Egypt and to all historical ages, covers the period from the creation of the world to the rise of Horus as king. From that time on,

Bronze mirror with handle fashioned in the form of a papyrus sceptre and the head of the goddess Hathor, later identified by the Greeks with Aphrodite. c. 1500 B.C.

Left: *Stela of the serpent king. The asp was emblematic of the king's invincible power and as such was widely revered by the Egyptians. As the* uraeus, *it was the distinctive mark of the pharaoh.*

Right: *Head of the Sphinx at Giza. Constructed from a single piece of rock in the reign of Khephren (c. 2650 B.C.) and probably fashioned in his likeness.*

Horus was to be ritually represented on earth by each successive pharaoh, whose rise to power was identified with that of Horus. Of the trials of Horus before he became king, we have a fairly full record, for his cult became bound up with that of Osiris and was therefore still of considerable importance when Egypt began to come in contact with the outside world and with such observers as Plutarch. Of the earlier part of the myth sequence we have less certain knowledge. But doctrinal differences between the four great cult centres hinged on their differing interpretations of the creation of the world. It seems more accurate to call the varying systems different interpretations rather than different beliefs, for the cults were generally regarded, certainly by the educated, as being different aspects of the same truths. Apparently the only group of priests who were at all dogmatic were those of Heliopolis, and their cult is the most completely known to us. The others were essentially variants of the Heliopolitan doctrine.

In the more sophisticated times of the New Kingdom (1546—1085 B.C.) at least it seems to have been recognised that the myths were a notation for spiritual ideas, a symbol language rather than a collection of stories. Educated men did not believe in the gods so much as in the forces that they represented; the animal attributes of the gods were a shorthand way of reminding the worshipper of the qualities of the god rather than indicating worship of the animal itself. The peasants may have taken these symbols more literally, but we know little of their beliefs. Certainly in later periods, when many religious benefits formerly reserved for the pharaoh or for the nobility were extended to the whole people, there is some evidence that this changed and the myths were treated as entertainment. But the Egyptians made no attempt to give myths logical formality, nor to reconcile all the inconsistencies resulting from superimposition of one cult on another. They may well have thought that a succession of fleeting images gave a better picture of the essentially unknowable. This is largely the technique even of the religious texts produced in the four great cult centres when expounding that part of their doctrine — the cosmogony — in which they specifically needed to make themselves clear in order to set themselves apart from their rivals. Instead, the priests of each cult centre seem to have borrowed aspects of their rivals' doctrine — perhaps in an attempt to be all-inclusive.

Above: *The sun's disk, enclosed by a snake, rests on the shoulders of two animals with the feather of truth on their heads. On the right is a mythical creature of the Underworld.*

Above right: *A papyrus painting showing the sun being rolled along its course by an enormous scarab accompanied by a religious procession.*

All the Egyptian cosmogonies are basically concerned with divinities of nature: the Sky, the Earth, the Sun and the Moon. The other gods which figure in the cosmogonies were possibly not originally connected with the creation legends, but were grafted on to the systems because of ethical or political considerations.

The Egyptians made the sky a goddess, Nut or Hathor, whom they represented either as a cow standing with her four feet planted on earth, or as a woman whose long, curved body touched the earth only with the tips of her toes and fingers. It was the starry belly of the goddess which men saw shining in the night above them. Sometimes also they imagined the sky as the head of a divine falcon whose eyes, which he opened and closed alternately, were the sun and the moon.

The earth, on the contrary, was a god, who was pictured lying prone and from whose back sprouted all the world's vegetation. The Egyptians called him Geb.

The sun, the most important of the Egyptian deities, had many names, and the interpretations given to his function were extremely varied.

OF THE WORLD

In his aspect of solar disk the sun was called Aten. When he rose he was called Khepri, when he climbed to the zenith he was called Ra, and when he set he was called Atum. He was also called Horus and it was under this name, joined with that of Ra, that he later reigned over all Egypt as Ra-Harakhte. It was claimed that he was reborn every morning of the celestial cow like a sucking calf, or like a little child of the sky-goddess. He was also said to be a falcon with speckled wings flying through space, or the right eye only of the great divine bird. Another conception of him was that of an egg laid daily by the celestial goose, 'the Great Cackler', or more frequently a gigantic scarab rolling before him the incandescent globe of the sun, just as on earth the sacred scarab rolls the ball of dung in which it has deposited its eggs.

The moon, too, was called by different names, the most important of which are Aah, Thoth and Khons. Sometimes he was considered to be the son of Nut, the sky-goddess. He was represented as a dog-headed ape, or as an ibis, or as the left eye of the great celestial falcon whose right eye was the sun.

Common concepts

The ancient Egyptians imagined that in the beginning the universe was filled with a primordial ocean called Nun. Though sometimes compared with a great waste of floodwaters and no doubt inspired by the Nile floodwaters, Nun had no surface: it completely filled the universe and could be likened to a cosmic egg. The waters of Nun were motionless, or stagnant; we do not know whether the Egyptians necessarily considered Nun to be potentially or inevitably life-bearing; certainly if we are to pursue the analogy with the Nile floodwaters, we can see that the Egyptians would have witnessed the apparently miraculous way in which as the floodwaters subside the pools they leave behind soon swarm with animal life. But we are given no clear indication of what the Egyptians thought had started the creative process: if it was immanent in Nun, which was featureless and eternal, why did creation in fact happen at a particular moment in the eternity of time?

Another concept held in common by all the

27

cosmogonies was that of the primeval hill rising out of Nun. The priests of each of the four great cult centres claimed that their temple stood on the site of this primeval hill; probably the first to make this claim were the Heliopolitans, but for their own prestige the other temples had to claim the same privilege for themselves. The first step-pyramids are doubtless symbolic representations of the primeval mound. It was sometimes imagined that, like the land emerging from the Nile floodwaters and eventually being inundated by them again, so the earth which had emerged from Nun might one day again be swallowed up into the primordial waste of waters.

Whatever details the Egyptians may have ascribed to the events and sequence of creation — and they tended to regard it as a slow development rather than as an instantaneous act of creation — they shared the view that what they called the 'First Time', or the age in which gods actually lived on earth and had their kingdoms there, was a golden age. Forces of destruction may have existed even then, but the principles of justice reigned over the land.

The Heliopolitan cosmogony

Though the Heliopolitan priests seem to have been the most doctrinaire, we have no clear exposition of their beliefs. The greatest religious document which has survived from Heliopolis, the *Pyramid Texts*, makes only passing references to creation, assuming basic knowledge of Heliopolitan doctrine.

It seems, however, that the first event in the creative process was the emergence of Atum, the god of Heliopolis, from the chaotic wastes of Nun. According to some texts, Atum created himself; according to others he was himself the child of Nun. He made his first appearance on the hill which was later to be surmounted by the temple of Heliopolis. According to other, earlier interpretations, Atum, whose name means something like the 'completed one', thus connecting him with creation, was himself the hill. Atum would then resemble the life-engendering hillocks left behind by the receding waters of the Nile. But as, by the time of the *Pyramid Texts*, Atum had become identified with the sun-god Ra, his emergence on the primeval hill was also interpreted as the coming of light to disperse the chaotic darkness of Nun. In this aspect Ra-Atum

Pectorals were attached to specified points on the mummified bodies of the dead. The one above has a hawk, vulture and uraeus motif and that on the right a scarab.

Right: *Woman with a lotus flower, a theme that recurs frequently although there is no evidence that it was a sacred emblem. Painted limestone stela from Sakkara. Fifth Dynasty.*

was symbolised by the phoenix, which alighted at dawn on the benben, an obelisk representing a ray of the sun. In another aspect, Ra-Atum was symbolised by the scarab beetle, pushing his egg out in front of him, thus starting with his appearance a cycle of creation. His name in this aspect was Khepri, 'He who becomes', later fixed as a symbol for the rising sun.

Atum was 'He who created himself'. His next act was to create further gods. As he was alone in the world, he had to produce offspring without a mate. His means, according to the earliest texts, was masturbation. This did not in any way appear to shock the Egyptians. Atum seems often in the texts to be regarded as a bisexual god and was sometimes called the 'Great He-She'. In a sense this legend seems to have provided a way for the Egyptians of intensifying his aspect of creative principle; conceiving of creation only in terms of sexual generation, the Egyptians were able through this episode in the myth to present Atum as a creative force which owed nothing to the agency of another. Atum gave birth to his son Shu by spitting him out, and to his daughter Tefnut by vomiting her forth. Shu's function as god of the air sprang naturally from the form of his birth; Tefnut seems to have had little significance in this case except as consort of Shu. But the priests' interpretations even at a fairly early date seem to have made Shu the life principle and Tefnut the principle of world order — called Mayet, the name of a formerly distinct goddess. Shu and Tefnut thus became suitable deities to carry on the creative cycle and establish a social order. Where these early events took place is uncertain. According to some texts Shu and Tefnut were created on the primeval mound. According to others, Atum remained in the waters of Nun and there created his son and daughter; Shu and Tefnut were brought up by Nun and looked after by Atum's Eye.

Atum seems only to have had one eye and it was physically separable from him and independent in its wishes. Important myths relate to this Eye, and a noteworthy one tells how Shu and Tefnut, still under Atum's protection, became separated from him in the dark wastes of the waters of Nun. Atum sent his Eye to look for them and eventually Shu and Tefnut came back with the Eye. Atum wept for joy, and from

his tears grew men. With the return of his children, Atum was ready to leave the waters of Nun and to enter the earth. But while the original Eye had been searching for Shu and Tefnut, Atum had replaced it with another, and much brighter one. The first Eye was enraged with Atum at finding himself supplanted when he returned. Atum therefore took the Eye and placed it on his forehead where it could rule the whole world which he was about to create. The Eye is often depicted as a destructive goddess — one aspect of the burning sun in Egypt, and it is associated with another destructive goddess, the rearing serpent which was in fact shown, in the form of the *uraeus* on the foreheads of the pharaohs, as a symbol of their power.

A section of the papyrus of Hent-Taui, a musician-priestess of Amon-Ra. The deceased is seen with Thoth who revealed to the dead the magic formulae needed to traverse the Underworld in safety. They are seen here adoring the sun disk, which contains the eye of Ra as it rises. Twenty-first Dynasty. British Museum.

Papyrus of Pa-Shebut-n-Mut, a musician-priestess of Amon-Ra. On the left the deceased and his soul in an attitude of worship. The god Shu, holding aloft the emblem of the sun disk, protects the soul on its voyage across the desert plateau. On the right are the four rudders of heaven. Twenty-first Dynasty. British Museum.

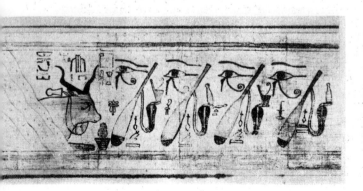

Shu and Tefnut became the parents of Geb, the earth, and his sister and wife Nut, the sky. With their birth, the divinities of the major aspects of nature were all accounted for. Geb and Nut were, however, the parents of four children who had no such cosmic associations. They were Isis and Osiris and Nephthys and Set. Horus, archetype of the pharaohs, was the son of Isis and Osiris, or was sometimes called the son of Nut. It may be that these five deities were incorporated into the Heliopolitan cosmogony by the priests, who wished to subordinate them to their own original gods. However that may be, this so-called Ennead of Heliopolis was a well-established tradition in the Egyptian religion, and the same family relationships are described in the literature of the other cult centres. Perhaps other cults were also incorporated but incompletely assimilated by the Heliopolitan priests, for other inconsistencies occur in their texts. An example is the confusion over the origin of Atum: generally he was considered to be self-created, but he is sometimes called the child of Nun, and this may be accounted for by an attempt by theologians to subordinate Atum to another legend which attributed the work of creation to Nun (perhaps here identified with the Nile).

Similarly some texts said that Horus was the son of Geb and Nut, and that he, together with his four brothers and sisters were jointly responsible for the procreation of the 'multitudes in the land', whereas in another Nut was called 'mother of the gods' and even 'she who bears Ra each day'. Atum is even described as setting Geb over the Ennead, which included himself. Indeed, the priests of Heliopolis considered themselves to be the representatives on earth of Geb and Nut, rather than of their chief god Atum. Again, in the *Pyramid Texts*, the Pharoah Pepi is declared in one passage to have been engendered by Atum before the creation of the earth, the heavens, men, gods and death; and in another passage he seems to be called the son of Nun: 'born in Nun before the creation of the heavens, earth, and the disorder and fear brought by the eye of Horus'. This hyperbole may of course not reflect the true Heliopolitan doctrine, but may merely be a poetic image or kind of magic incantation designed to ensure the safe passage of the king's soul to the after world by asserting his divine origin.

The Memphite cosmogony

Very early in the historical period, in about 3100 B.C., Upper and Lower Egypt were joined for the first time with the capital of the united country at Memphis, near the apex of the Nile delta. The city was founded by the first pharaoh, Menes. Older cities, such as Heliopolis, were not far distant from Memphis, and it no doubt therefore seemed particularly important to the early rulers to assert the superiority of Memphis, not merely as the seat of the centralised government and thus of prime political importance, but also as a religious centre superior to all others in the land. The political background goes a long way towards explaining the particular form taken by the cosmogony of Memphis.

Ptah, the high god of Memphis and god as the master of destiny, was declared to be the creator of the world. The whole Heliopolitan cosmogony was not thereby set aside entirely, but it was claimed that the deities of the Heliopolitan Ennead were merely manifestations of the supreme god Ptah. The Shabaka Stone, a late copy on stone of an early text, which is the source of our knowledge of Memphite theology, is very clear on this point. The tone of the Shabaka Stone text is polemical: it seems to take each point of the Heliopolitan beliefs in order almost to turn it upside down. This reinforces our belief that the priests of Memphis were concerned, for the glory of their own city, to deny a more widely held view of creation.

The Shabaka Stone declares that Ptah is he who sits upon the Great Throne: he is therefore identified with the Great God who, like the Great Mother, was a deity early worshipped in Egypt, perhaps as a fertility-god. Ptah was then declared to be Nun, the Father, who begat Atum, and also (the female form of Nun) Naunet, the Mother, who bore Atum. The text goes on to say that Ptah is the Heart and the Tongue of the Ennead (i.e. of Heliopolis). The heart and the tongue were generally considered by the Egyptians to be respectively the seats of the mind or intelligence and of command or power; they were therefore regarded as symbols of Atum, the creator. In the Memphite system Atum was thus merely the agent of Ptah's will, who understood his commands and carried them out. Atum spat forth Shu and vomited out Tefnut; but these, too, seem to be identified with Heart and Tongue, and are therefore also only aspects of Ptah's creative will. We have already seen that Tefnut was sometimes identified with the goddess

Left: *Bronze figure of Ptah. According to Memphite theology, Ptah was the creator of the universe. He is usually represented in mummy bandages.*

Right: *Head of a queen wearing a diadem in the form of a griffin with the royal* uraeus *on either side. Granite. Eighteenth Dynasty.*

The ancient Egyptian believed that his gods shared his own material needs. Offerings of food, drink and riches were therefore an important part of religion. This bearer carries papyrus stems and jars containing libations (usually of beer, milk, oil or wine).

Mayet, the spirit of world order. Thus Ptah was also seen as the establisher of a moral order and of royal power. Horus, an aspect of Ptah and personified in ritual as the reigning pharaoh, is declared, in the Shabaka Stone to be ruler of the land and responsible for uniting it and naming it with the great name Tatenen. Now Tatenen was the name given in Memphis to Ptah ('Ptah of the primeval mound'), and the passage would therefore signify that Ptah not only created the land, but also that he *was* the land (just as in some versions Atum was declared actually to be the primeval mound, not simply to have been created on it). This, incidentally, was intended to confute the Heliopolitan claim that their temple stood on the primeval mound.

The Memphite theologians seem to have been aware that these personifications of Ptah were only symbols for quasi-philosophical ideas: that Ptah was the creative principle which acts through thought and will or command. In a variant of the Memphite system, Atum is relegated to further insignificance; according to this version Atum is replaced as the agent of Ptah's will by Horus, who is the Heart, and by Thoth, who is the Tongue. This seems to be an attempt to incorporate even earlier beliefs than the Heliopolitan, for Horus was an ancient sun-god and Thoth the moon-god and the god of wisdom.

Ptah of Memphis was not only the universal and sole creator of the physical world, absorbing the functions of all the other gods; he also created an ethical order. In this respect the Memphite cosmogony seems to be more far-reaching than the Heliopolitan — but our knowledge of the latter may be incomplete. We are not told any more about Ptah's creative activity, but the Shabaka Stone text states that Ptah created everything, including the gods, and that he was also the origin of all good things — food and drink, offerings to the gods and every divine utterance (equivalent to divine acts of creation). It was recognised that his power was greater than that of all the other gods. He set the gods (who were, of course, aspects of his own divinity) in the places where their cults were practised; he established what offerings were to be made to them; he founded their shrines; and he created out of all the materials of his own being (i.e. the earth) the forms or images in which they were worshipped. The gods then entered into these forms and were contented to rule together with their creator Ptah, Lord of the Two Lands. Ptah also established the cities and founded the nomes (provinces of Egypt), thus creating a political order.

Ptah was sometimes called the Divine Artificer as he was the supreme creator, and he was identified by the Greeks with their own god Hephaestus. But his function seems rather to have been as Lord of Truth; he is everywhere accompanied by Thoth, god of wisdom, and his works are the works of justice. 'Whereas he makes all things in a perfect manner, not deceptively, but artificially, together with Truth, he is called Ptah.'

The Memphite priests attempted also to associate their city with the Osiris cult, which was to gain such prominence, by claiming that Memphis was the site of a crucial episode in the Osiris legend. As Osiris, like Ptah, was supposed to have taught mankind the arts of civilisation, it may be that the Memphite priests were attempting to assimilate Osiris within their own system.

The Hermopolitan cosmogony

In Hermopolis, a city of Upper Egypt, a quite distinctive theory of creation was held which, it was claimed, was evolved earlier than any of the other cosmogonies. For the Heliopolitan Ennead, the Hermopolitans substituted an Ogdoad, or group of eight gods. These were Nun and his consort Naunet, Huh and his consort Hauhet, Kuk and his consort Kauket and Amon and his consort Amaunet. These eight gods together created the world. They then ruled over it for a period which was considered to be a Golden Age. After they had reigned for some time and they had completed their work of creation, the Eight died and went to the Underworld to live. Their power persisted after their death, however, for they continued to cause the Nile to flow and the sun to rise each day.

Two of the Hermopolitan Ogdoad, Nun and Amon, also figure in the other cosmogonies. The name of each of the goddesses is simply the feminine form of the name of the god whose consort she is; we may therefore treat these divinities as being only four in number. Etymologically, the names seem to have the following significance: Nun, water; Huh, unendingness; Kuk, darkness; and Amon, that which is unseen, or air. The four deities may therefore be considered to personify elements in the creation legends concerning Nun which were told in the other cult centres. Nun was there described as an infinite watery waste, chaotic and dark. Amon, if he is to be regarded in the Hermopolitan legend as air or wind, would then represent the force which stirred up the waters out of their stagnant immobility. The power of creation was thus immanent in Nun, but Amon was the essential force which set in motion the creative cycle.

The four male deities of the Ogdoad were depicted in Egyptian art with frogs' heads, and the four female deities had serpents' heads. This would seem to derive from another tradition in Hermopolis which likened the eight primordial gods to the amphibious life which swarmed, apparently self-created, in the mud left behind by the annually receding Nile floodwaters. Thus instead of creating the primeval mound, the Eight would be conceived as hatching out on to it.

As in the other cult centres, the city was declared to be on the site of the primeval hill. In a park attached to the temple was a sacred lake called the 'Sea of the Two Knives' from which emerged the 'Isle of Flames'. This island was

A limestone tablet dedicated to Thoth, god of letters and scribe of the Underworld, and one of the earliest deities. Usually represented as an ibis, he is also god of the moon and is seen here with a winged moon over his head. British Museum.

said to be the primeval hill, and was a great place of pilgrimage and the setting for much ritual. Four variants of the creation myth as told at Hermopolis are connected with this lake and this island. In the first, the world was said to have originated in a cosmic egg (a concept not unlike that of the all-embracing Nun) which was laid by a celestial goose, which first broke the silence of the world, and was known as the 'Great Cackler'. The egg, laid on the primeval mound, contained the bird of light, Ra, who was to be the creator of the world. Other sources say that the egg contained air — a tradition more in keeping with the Ogdoad legend. The remains of the egg were shown to pilgrims at Hermopolis. The second version is similar to the first, except that in this case the egg was laid by an ibis — the bird sacred to Thoth, god of the moon and of wisdom. The cult of Thoth at Hermopolis was certainly established later than that of the Ogdoad, and it has therefore been suggested that this myth is an attempt by the

Hermopolitan priests to graft the Thoth legend on to the older Ogdoad legend. The third variant of the Hermopolitan doctrine reverts to the imagery of creation out of the waters, and is exceptionally poetic. According to this version, a lotus flower rises out of the waters of the 'Sea of the Two Knives'. When its petals open the calix of the flower is seen to bear a divine child, who is Ra. Another version of this legend is that the lotus opens to reveal a scarab beetle (symbol of the sun); the scarab then transforms itself into a boy, who weeps; and finally, his tears become mankind. This is another way of saying that men are the children of Ra. The lotus is a flower which opens and closes every day: it could therefore easily be associated with the cult of the sun-god, which it bore within its petals.

The Ogdoad were said to be responsible for the flow of the Nile and the daily rise of the sun; they were also said to have created the lotus bearing the sun-god and this lotus rose out of the waters — always a source of fecundity in Egypt and in this case no doubt associated with the waters of Nun. It may be seen, therefore, that these myths are easily reconciled with each other and constitute poetic variants rather than conflicting stories. Not even Hermopolitan legend, however, is without anomalies. Thus the texts state that 'out of the lotus, created by the Eight, came forth Ra, who created *all things*, divine and human'.

The Theban cosmogony

The chief god of Thebes, a city of Upper Egypt, which was the seat of the centralised government in the New Kingdom (1546—1085 B.C.) was called Amon. The gods of the other chief cult centres had already become established as high gods throughout Egypt and had considerable popularity among the people, who by this time had come to share in the benefits of the formerly exclusive religion. It was therefore essential for the priests of Thebes, if they were to command support for the advance of their deity to the position of chief god, that they should incorporate the main features of all the earlier cosmogonies.

Amon, who also figured in the Hermopolitan myths, was associated with the air as an invisible, dynamic force; it was thus easy to identify him with the power of the supreme and invisible creator. Theban doctrine incorporated in Amon aspects of all the other creator gods. It stated that Thebes was the first city, after which all the others were later modelled. Thebes was the site of the first water, i.e. Nun, and of the first land, i.e. the primeval mound. The city was founded on the hill and in this way the earth began. Then mankind was created in order to found other cities after the pattern of Thebes. Thebes was the Eye of Ra, and it oversaw all the other cities (just as the Eye of Atum oversaw the twins Shu and Tefnut).

Like Atum, Amon created himself: there was no other god to create him, and he had neither

Amon, Mut and Khons, the Great Triad of Thebes. Amon wears a double-feathered head-dress, Mut the white crown of Upper Egypt. Khons holds the emblems of life, stability and purity, with the flagellum and crook of Osiris.

36

Hypostyle of the Rameseum or Memnonium, the mortuary temple of Rameses II at Thebes. Here are records of the Pharaoh's military achievements which throw much light on contemporary methods of waging war. Nineteenth Dynasty.

father nor mother. He was invisible, born in secret. All the other gods came into being after he had performed the first creative act. Just as Ptah was said to embody other gods as facets of his own divine nature, so the Theban Amon embraced whole cosmogonies as aspects or phases of his creative activity. Thus the first of his forms was said to be the Ogdoad of Hermopolis; his next form was as Tatenen, the primeval mound of Memphis, in which form he created the first gods. Amon then left the earth to abide in heaven as Ra (a Hermopolitan belief). He also took the form of the divine child revealed by the opening petals of the lotus in the midst of Nun. Like Ra or Horus, his eyes lit the earth. He made men and created the gods, organising the Ennead and setting up the members of the Ogdoad as his divine fathers and priests, with Shu at their head and Tefnut as the concubine of the god. As in Hermopolitan belief, Amon was the vital force which roused Nun from his torpor and started the creative cycle.

The priests of Thebes also claimed that their city was the birthplace of Osiris, no doubt because by this time Osiris had attained such popularity and was associated with the well-being of the royal house and the fertility of the land.

37

Other cosmogonic notions

Like many primitive peoples, the ancient Egyptians seem early on to have worshipped a universal mother-goddess. She took many forms, and her tradition can be traced in a number of goddesses who survived into the pantheon of historical times. The background of a mother-goddess tradition often explains the particular form taken by myths in which these goddesses were involved. It may well be that this deity was supposed to have been the creator of the entire world. Thus Nut, or Hathor, is said to have been the mother of Ra; Geb was her bull and Ra their son; men, in turn, were sometimes called the 'cattle of Ra'. Alternatively, Hathor's son is the 'bull of confusion' Ihy who, having only one parent, is similar to Shu. Ihy was a symbol of a fresh beginning. Again Isis, though originally only the consort of Osiris, was made the mother of Horus, from whom are descended all the pharaohs — on whom in turn the lives of all his subjects depend. Neith, the goddess of Sais, in the Delta, was no doubt also such a deity, though she was primarily a warlike goddess. She is referred to as the oldest of the deities, and as such the gods appeal to her for judgment during the Great Quarrel between Set and Horus.

Khnum, a god perhaps later absorbed by Amon, but who survived as an independent deity in Elephantine, near the First Cataract of the Nile, was said to have created men from clay and to have fashioned them on a potter's wheel. This would mean that mankind, together with the entire animal world, had emerged from the sun-dried mud of the Nile, thus by-passing the agency of the gods of the Ennead.

Right: *Wooden stela dedicated to and depicting Ra-Harakhte.*

A statue of the goddess Neith, one of the guardians of coffins and Canopic jars. She is also known as the war-goddess of Sais, and is usually represented, as here, wearing the red crown of Lower Egypt. Later identified by the Greeks with Athena.

Left: *Isis holding a sistrum. Temple of Seti I at Abydos.*

Euergetes II pouring a libation before Haroeris and Tafner (Haroeris' wife). Temple at Kom Ombo. 41

THE DEITIES

Like all peoples in antiquity the Egyptians explained everything by the intervention of a god, and for them there was nothing which was not capable of containing supernatural power. Consequently the number of gods worshipped in the Nile valley was considerable, and a list found in the tomb of Thuthmosis III enumerates no fewer than seven hundred and forty. Of most of them we know only the names and it would serve no useful purpose to list them here. We shall limit this study to those deities who enjoyed a genuine cult or who occupied a real place in Egyptian mythology.

Left: *Coloured relief of Rameses II in the Great Temple at Abu Simbel. The pharaoh is being embraced by a goddess, probably Isis.*

Right: *Osiris, god of the Underworld and judge of the dead, whose cult was centred at Abydos, and postulated a life after death which could be attained not only by the pharaoh but by all. The dead man underwent a judgment in the presence of forty-two assessors, and if declared 'true of voice' was led into the presence of Osiris.*

43

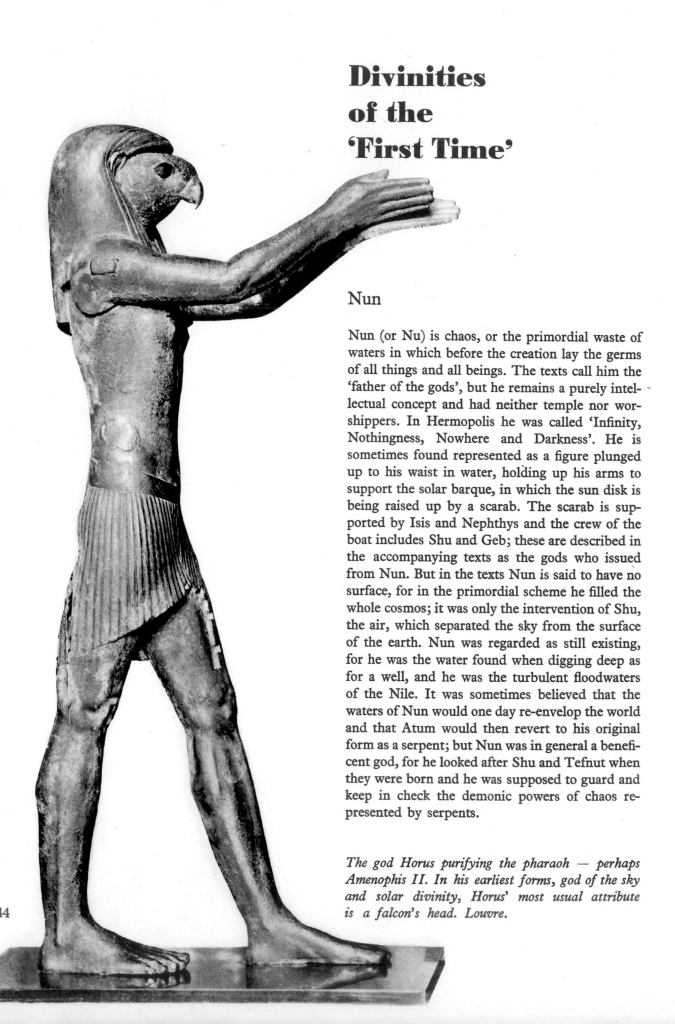

Divinities of the 'First Time'

Nun

Nun (or Nu) is chaos, or the primordial waste of waters in which before the creation lay the germs of all things and all beings. The texts call him the 'father of the gods', but he remains a purely intellectual concept and had neither temple nor worshippers. In Hermopolis he was called 'Infinity, Nothingness, Nowhere and Darkness'. He is sometimes found represented as a figure plunged up to his waist in water, holding up his arms to support the solar barque, in which the sun disk is being raised up by a scarab. The scarab is supported by Isis and Nephthys and the crew of the boat includes Shu and Geb; these are described in the accompanying texts as the gods who issued from Nun. But in the texts Nun is said to have no surface, for in the primordial scheme he filled the whole cosmos; it was only the intervention of Shu, the air, which separated the sky from the surface of the earth. Nun was regarded as still existing, for he was the water found when digging deep as for a well, and he was the turbulent floodwaters of the Nile. It was sometimes believed that the waters of Nun would one day re-envelop the world and that Atum would then revert to his original form as a serpent; but Nun was in general a beneficent god, for he looked after Shu and Tefnut when they were born and he was supposed to guard and keep in check the demonic powers of chaos represented by serpents.

The god Horus purifying the pharaoh — perhaps Amenophis II. In his earliest forms, god of the sky and solar divinity, Horus' most usual attribute is a falcon's head. Louvre.

44

Atum

Atum (or Tem or Tum) whose name seems to come from a root which signified 'not to be' and 'to be complete', was originally a local god of Heliopolis, where his sacred animal was the bull Merwer (Greek, Mnevis). From very early times his priests identified him with Ra, the great sun-god. They taught that inside Nun, before the creation, there had lived a 'spirit, still formless, who bore within him the sum of all existence'. He was called Atum, and he manifested himself one day under the name of Ra-Atum and drew from himself gods, men and all living things.

Later, Atum was personified as the setting sun and the sun before its rising. His cult spread widely through Egypt, conjointly with that of Ra, though the role of both was to change owing to the rival claims of other gods and other cults.

Atum was ordinarily considered to be the ancestor of the human race. He is always represented with a man's head, wearing the double crown of the pharaohs — the 'pschent'. Originally unmarried, Atum was supposed to have fathered the first divine couple — Shu and Tefnut — without the aid of a wife. Only later was he given a spouse — indeed two, for at Memphis he was united sometimes with Iusas and sometimes with Nebhet Hotep, who was said to have borne him the twin gods Shu and Tefnut.

Ra

Ra (or Re or Phra), which probably signifies 'Creator', is the name of the sun, sovereign lord of the sky. He had his principal sanctuary at Heliopolis. The priests of this city affirmed that it was here that Ra first manifested himself on the primeval hill which rose from Nun in the stone object in the form of an obelisk, which represented a sun's ray. The obelisk was called the benben stone and was piously preserved in the temple named for this reason Het Benben — the 'palace of the obelisk'.

Formerly, according to the priests of Heliopolis, the sun-god reposed, under the name of Atum, in the bosom of Nun, the primordial ocean. There, in order that his flame should run no risk of being extinguished, he took care to keep his eyes shut. He enclosed himself in the bud of a lotus (this would seem to be borrowed from Hermopolitan belief) until the day when, weary of his own impersonality, he rose by an effort of will from the abyss and appeared in glittering splendour under the name of Ra. He then bore Shu and Tefnut who, in their turn, gave birth to Geb and Nut, from whom issued Osiris and Isis, Set and Nephthys. These are the eight great divinities who with their chief Ra — or more exactly Ra-Atum, since Ra and Atum were identified with each other — form the divine company or Ennead of Heliopolis.

Ra drew from himself, and without recourse to woman, the first divine couple. It is not until much later that he was given as his spouse Rat — which is only his own name feminised — or Iusas, Eus-os, Uert-Hekeu, 'the great of magic'. As for the other gods, men and all other living creatures, it was said that they came from Ra's sweat and from his tears — perhaps a play on words since 'tears' and 'men' have a similar sound in Egyptian.

At the same time Ra had created a first universe, different from the present world, and known to the Egyptians as the 'First Time', a Golden Age. During the 'First Time' men and gods lived together on the earth and Ra governed it from the 'Prince's Palace' in Heliopolis, where he normally resided. The *Pyramid Texts* minutely describe for us his royal existence and how, after his morning toilet and meal, he would get into his sacred barque and, accompanied by his scribe, Weneg, inspect the twelve provinces of his kingdom, spending one of the twelve hours of daylight in each province.

As long as Ra remained young and vigorous he reigned peacefully over gods and men; but the years brought with them their ravages and the texts depict him as an old man with trembling mouth from which saliva ceaselessly dribbles. We shall see later how Isis took advantage of the god's senility, made him reveal his secret name and thus acquired sovereign power.

Even men perceived Ra's decrepitude and began to murmur against him, saying: 'His Majesty is grown old. His bones are silver, his flesh gold and his hair real lapis lazuli.' The plots of mankind against him finally reached Ra's ears. Justly enraged, he summoned his council and, having consulted the gods one by one on the measures which should be taken, he decided to hurl his divine Eye against his rebellious subjects, for the Eye of Ra or Atum was a separable entity with a mind of its own. Later we shall tell how the divine Eye (taking the form of the goddess Hathor) rushed upon the guilty and massacred them without pity until Ra, appeased, managed to put an end to the bloodshed; for his goodness would not permit him to allow the entire human race to be exterminated.

This was not, however, the end of Ra's troubles. On another occasion, the Eye wandered away and Ra sent Thoth to fetch it back; when the Eye, or the sun, returned to Ra it found to its fury that it had been replaced by another Eye (perhaps the moon). Thoth, however, mollified the original Eye, and Ra pacified it by placing it, in the shape of the *uraeus* serpent, on his forehead 'where it could rule the whole world'. This evidently is a variant of the other myth already recounted, that the Eye became enraged to find itself supplanted when it returned to Atum after seeking Shu and Tefnut in the dark waters of Nun; on that occasion the Eye was not merely placated by being placed on Atum's forehead, it was being rewarded for its help in finding and bringing back Shu and Tefnut. In both cases the significance of the legend is clear: the Eye, or *uraeus* serpent, was to become the effective ruler of the world, and as such was to be worn by the pharaohs as a symbol of their majesty and of their descent from the sun-god.

The ingratitude of men had inspired in Ra a distaste for the world and a desire to withdraw himself beyond reach. (This again may be the significance of Ra's delegation of power to the Eye.) So, on the orders of Nun, the goddess Nut changed herself into a cow and took Ra on her back. She raised him high into the vault of heaven and at the same time, as we shall later relate, the present world was created. The sun-god Ra abdicated his position as ruler of the world in favour of the moon-god Thoth, who brought light back to mankind. This was how the Egyptians explained the daily disappearance of the sun in the evening and its replacement by the moon.

From the time when Ra retired to the heavens, a fixed order was established for him. The world was bounded by mountains which supported the sky and at whose foot was Naunet, the consort of Nun in Hermopolitan doctrine. It was from these mountains that Ra appeared. The sun was therefore reborn daily either from the watery abyss or alternatively as son of the sky-goddess. He emerged in the east from behind Manu, the mountain of sunrise, and began his journey across the sky in what was called the Manjet-boat, or 'barque of millions of years'. Ra is accompanied by a number of gods who act as the boat's crew. These include Geb and Thoth and the personifications of various aspects of the sun's power, especially those of authoritative utterance, i.e. command and creation by divine (or royal) decree, of intelligence and of magic. Horus is also sometimes a member of the crew, standing at the helm of the boat while Thoth stands at its prow destroying all Ra's enemies. As he sails across the sky, Ra wears the double crown of Egypt, which combines the red crown of Lower Egypt and the white crown of Upper Egypt. As on the crown of the pharaohs, the *uraeus* serpent is seen at the front of the crown rearing its head and spitting fire at all enemies.

The chief of Ra's enemies was Apep, or Apophis, a huge serpent who lived in the waters of Nun or in the depths of the celestial Nile and who each day attempted to obstruct the passage of the solar barque. This was a serious challenge to Ra, and it has been suggested that in this legend Apep represents the earlier and discarded form of the sun-god himself, when he was lying in the waters of Nun before he began the creation of the world. This would explain Apep's strength and his particular resentment of the daily journey of the sun across the sky; it would also explain why in these daily battles Ra was always ultimately victorious. In the myth of the Great Quarrel, Set claims that it is he who stands in the prow of the solar barque and vanquishes all the enemies of Ra and casts them back into the abyss. Stormy weather would be interpreted by the Egyptians as a momentary victory of the serpent Apep. Likewise when there was a total eclipse the Egyptians thought Apep had swallowed the solar barque.

It was sometimes thought that Ra was born in the morning as a child, grew to maturity by midday, and by evening had become a doddering old man who would die that night. This legend corresponded to the myth of his reign on earth.

Accordingly, when Ra embarked on his night voyage he was given the name Auf, which means 'flesh' or 'corpse'. For his journey through the twelve hours of darkness Ra sailed in another boat, the Mesektet-boat or night-barque. This boat was sometimes represented as a serpent with a head at either end. As during the day, Ra is accompanied by a crew of gods, which again include the personifications of authoritative utterance and of intelligence. During the night, the god Upuaut, Opener of Roads, stands at the prow of the barque.

Adoration of Ra at his rising in the east. Below him is the tat, *the four-barred symbol of stability which represents Osiris. From the papyrus of Hunefer, Theban Book of the Dead. Early Nineteenth Dynasty. British Museum.*

Above: *Bronze seated figure of Ra, the great sun-god, with the solar disk on his head and a papyrus sceptre. British Museum.*

According to another belief, the stars formed the crew of the solar barques. 'Those who can never set' are the stars which do not set during the day but are invisible because of the sun's brilliance; they form the day crew. 'Those who can never become weary' are the stars which are visible for only a short time during the night; these are the night crew and they are imagined to slip away one by one towards the West (the Underworld to the Egyptians) where they join the night-barque in its journey through the invisible part of the world, which is called Det.

During the twelve hours of the night the perils which Ra faced were even greater than those he faced during the day. Again he is confronted by his eternal enemy, the serpent Apep. But in the Underworld each of the twelve provinces which Ra must visit during the hours of darkness is peopled by monstrous serpents and demons who threaten the existence of the dead as personified in the dead sun-god Auf. Like the souls of dead human beings, the previous forms of the sun-god, Atum, Ra and Khepri, are said to be buried in the Underworld. As Auf passes along the infernal river, the various gods and demons which inhabit each province of the Underworld come forward to tow his barque. But these are not friendly spirits. They are monstrous creatures which take the forms of serpents with two heads at either end, as in the fourth province, or of a huge serpent whose back bears the heads of four bearded men. This last serpent, which inhabited the sixth province, was called the 'devourer of spirits' and was said to be invisible to Auf. The four men on his back were the sons of Horus, Imset, Hapy, Duamutef and Qebehsenuf, which were the spirits presiding over the Canopic jars in which after embalmment the lungs, liver, stomach and intestines of a dead man were preserved. The serpent himself was said to devour the defeated enemies of Ra and Osiris. This brief description of the inhabitants of one of the twelve provinces will give some idea of mysterious terror and invisible perils represented by the realm of the Underworld in the solar myths; as we shall see when we consider the Osiris cult, the Underworld was later to become a realm where a man might hope for eternal life. But even when these beliefs prevailed, spells and magic incantations had to be said by the living to preserve the dead soul from the threatening demons by which it was

The four Canopic jars carried the heads of the four sons of Horus, the Amenti, genii of the lower world. After embalming, the viscera were placed in their respective jars. Imset received the liver, Qebehsenuf (below) the intestines, jackal-headed Duamutef (below right) the stomach, and Hapy the lungs.

attacked on its passage. Part of the role of Auf in the Underworld was briefly to shed light on the souls of the dead as he passed through their realm. He would pass from cavern to cavern, receiving the acclamations of the inhabitants of the Underworld, who waited with impatience for the light he bore and after his departure fell back into the agony of darkness.

Having overcome all the perils of the Underworld, including the serpent Apep, the sun-god reaches the twelfth province and rises once more to shine upon the earth. The gods of his retinue drag up his barque (the Manjet-boat), and as Khepri the sun-god rises once more into the sky. The form of Auf is discarded and is seen lying to the side. Shu, the god of the air, is seen ready to take the sun's disk into his outstretched arms, just as at evening the solar disk is handed from one boat to another by the goddess of the east to the goddess of the west.

Such were the most widely held ideas about the daily solar cycle; but other notions persisted, perhaps chiefly among the common people. One was that Ra was the son of the sky-goddess, Nut, who was represented by a cow. Ra was imagined as a calf born anew every morning and swallowed up by his mother, the sky-goddess every evening. This would explain why when Ra-Atum decided to withdraw from the world after the near-destruction of mankind, he was borne up to the heavens by the cow-goddess Nut. The sun was also imagined sometimes to be the son of Nun: in Hermopolitan doctrine he was said to rise each morning from the opening petals of a lotus flower floating on the waters of Nun, and as the petals of the lotus closed again in the evening Ra would be enfolded within them.

The forms and names of Ra are innumerable and the *Litanies of the Sun*, engraved at the entrance of the royal tombs, enumerate no fewer than seventy-five. One of the most important is as a figure with the head of a falcon, surmounted by a disk bearing the *uraeus*, the terrible sacred serpent who is described as spitting flames which destroy the god's enemies. This is Ra-Harakhte, the great solar god of Heliopolis, sovereign lord of Egypt, and represents a combination of the god Ra with a former high god of Egypt, Horus, who either was the sun or whose right eye was the sun. As the sun during his voyage through the hours of darkness, the god was

49

Khepri

represented by Auf-Ra, a man with the head of a ram. This ram symbol may have been taken from the sacred ram of Mendes, which was considered to be the soul of Osiris. Other representations were as a divine child lying in the calix of a lotus flower, as the Bennu bird, or phoenix, which rose at dawn from the benben stone and with its voice heralded the good tidings of creation, as the bull Merwer, or simply as a man, seated or walking, whose head is surmounted by the solar disk around which is wreathed the *uraeus*. Originally, however, only Atum was represented as a human being.

Universally recognised as the creator and ruler of the world, Ra, with whom all the other gods were finally identified, became from the time of the Old Kingdom the divinity particularly revered by the pharaohs, who not only wore Ra's symbol of divine authority, the Eye, or *uraeus* serpent, but also claimed to be actually the sons of Ra. One story tell us how the sun-god came to Reddedet, the high priest's wife, in the guise of her husband and how from this union were born the three first kings of the Fifth Dynasty. Each time that a pharaoh was conceived, Ra was said to have returned to earth to espouse the queen. Thus the pharaohs were able to claim not only that they had been handed down their authority in direct succession from Horus (i.e. Horus the sun, not Horus son of Osiris), but that they were so closely linked with the sun that their line partook of the sun's inevitable rebirth after death. Royal commands were thus of divine authority; as he was sole mediator between Ra and the people of Egypt, the pharaoh could expect that the people would take very seriously their duty to ensure by prayers that his soul passed safely through the perils of the Underworld. For just as it was essential for the fertility and well-being of the land of Egypt and its peoples that the sun should rise every morning, so it was essential that the soul of the dead pharaoh should be protected and that his son, the new incarnation of Ra, should be equally respected.

Of the celebrated sanctuary of Heliopolis, where the god was worshipped in the form of a gigantic obelisk — a petrified sun's ray called the benben stone — and where he used to take the form of the bull Merwer, or, at times, the bird Bennu, there remain today only shapeless ruins and an obelisk, the oldest in Egypt.

Khepri (or Khepera) signifies at the same time 'scarab' and 'He who becomes'. We see him represented in many fashions. The scarab can be seen pushing along in front of it a ball of food which it buries in order to be able to eat it unmolested. The Egyptians thought that this ball was the egg which the female scarab lays in a ball of her own dung. They therefore took the scarab as a symbol for the self-generative aspect of the sun-god, for they conceived of the scarab as being born out of itself. Khepri thus represented the rising sun which, like the scarab, emerges from its own substance and is reborn of itself. He was the god of the transformations which life, for ever renewing itself, manifests. He is represented as a scarab-faced man, or as a man whose head is surmounted by this insect. Sometimes the god appears simply as a scarab.

Shu

Shu, who with Tefnut his twin sister comprised the first couple of the Ennead, was created by Ra without recourse to woman. His name derives from a verb which means 'to raise' and can be translated as 'he who holds up'. He is the Atlas of Egyptian mythology and supports the sky. It was told of him how, on the orders of Ra, he slipped between his two children, Geb the earth-god and Nut, goddess of the sky, who had until then been closely united. He threw them violently apart and elevated Nut high into the air, where he maintained her with his upraised arms. One version of this story tells how Shu separated Geb and Nut on his own initiative, for he was in love with his daughter and jealous of Geb's union with her.

Shu is also the god of air. In some texts he seems to be treated as emptiness deified; in others he is accorded rather more importance. As god of air, Shu is seen in the later texts as personifying the divine intelligence. He therefore becomes the immediate agent of Atum's creation, and hence an embodiment of Atum's supreme power. Shu thus becomes the god who set creation in motion, forming the world by separating earth and sky. From this legend arose some dispute as to whether Nun, Atum or Shu was the oldest of the gods, and some Egyptian theologians seem to have thought that all three were born simultaneously.

Shu, like Atum, is always represented in human form. On his head he normally wears, as a distinctive sign, an ostrich feather — which is the hieroglyph of his name.

Though Thoth was sometimes said to have succeeded Ra as king on earth, Shu was more generally thought to have been his father's successor. But, like his father, Shu experienced the vicissitudes of power; for the children of Apep plotted against him and attacked him in his palace of At Nub. He vanquished them, but disease riddled him, so that even his faithful followers revolted. Weary of reigning, Shu abdicated in favour of his son Geb and took refuge in the skies.

Left: Two representations of Anhur, the human-headed god of war and divine huntsman. The right-hand figure shows him wearing a plume of four hawk's feathers. Twenty-first Dynasty. c. 700 B.C.

Tefnut

Tefnut seems to have been a theological concept rather than a real person. At Heliopolis she was said to be Shu's twin sister and wife, but she appears to have been paired in earlier times with a certain god Tefen, of whom we know nothing but the name. In the Memphite cosmogony, as we have seen, Tefnut acquired a more positive character, and was identified with the Tongue of Ptah, or symbol of the means to creation; in this function she partnered her brother Shu as an embodiment of the supreme divine power. Alternatively, Tefnut was sometimes identified with the goddess Mayet, the spirit of world order, whereby she acquired an even more positive spiritual significance.

Goddess of the dew and the rain, it seems she also had a solar character. She was worshipped in the form of a lioness or of a woman with the head of a lioness, and the Greeks sometimes identified her with Artemis. She is depicted in the texts as a pale copy of Shu, whom she helps to support the sky and with whom each morning she receives the new-born sun as it breaks free from the eastern mountains.

Anhur

Anhur (the Greek rendering is 'Onuris') seems to signify 'He who leads what has gone away' but has also been translated as 'Sky-bearer'. God of Sebennytus and This, it is believed that he symbolised the creative power of the sun. He was very soon identified with Shu and invoked under the name Anhur-Shu. He is assumed to be a warlike personification of Ra, and was identified by the Greeks as Ares, the god of battle.

He is represented with the traits of a warrior wearing a head-dress adorned with four tall straight plumes. He is covered by a long embroidered robe and often brandishes a lance. Sometimes he holds the cord by which he leads the sun. Legend recounts how once the Eye of Ra fled from Egypt and was brought back from Nubia by Anhur. This story, like the others concerning the losing and finding of the Eye, ends with the Eye becoming enraged upon seeing that another Eye had taken its place and with Ra setting it on his forehead as the *uraeus*.

Anhur was very popular under the New Kingdom and was called 'the Saviour' and 'the Good

Warrior'. He was fervently invoked against enemies and against noxious animals, whom he hunted without respite from his chariot. His popularity was of long duration; for Herodotus speaks of the great festivals he saw celebrated at Papremis and tells us of the innumerable cudgel blows which priests and the faithful enthusiastically exchanged in honour of their god. As a wife he was given Mehit, who seems to be a mere double of Tefnut, the sister-wife of Shu. She was worshipped at This, and is pictured as a lion-headed goddess.

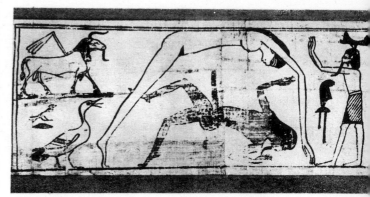

Geb

Geb (or Seb or Keb) constituted with Nut the second in the Ennead. Plutarch identifies him with Cronus. In reality he was the earth-god, the physical foundation of the world; but in classical times he scarcely had anything resembling a cult.

We have already seen how Geb had been separated by Shu from Nut, his sister-spouse. Since that time he had remained inconsolable and his lamentations could be heard night and day.

Geb is often represented lying under the feet of Shu, against whom he had vainly struggled to defend his wife. Raised on one elbow, with one knee bent, he thus symbolises the mountains and the undulations of the earth's crust. His body is sometimes covered with verdure.

Geb is nearly always depicted as a man without any special attributes, but on occasion his head is surmounted by a goose, which is the hieroglyph of his name. Certain legends, moreover, describe him as a gander, the 'Great Cackler', whose female laid the cosmic egg containing the sun. Others make him a vigorous bull who has fertilised the celestial cow, 'the bull of Nut'.

Most frequently, however, Geb was reputed to be the father — and Nut the mother — of the Osirian gods, and for this reason was known as the 'father of the gods'. Another explanation for this appellation is seen by scholars to lie in Nut's ancient role as mother-goddess. Nut could on this account easily be thought of as 'mother of the gods', and her husband in the Heliopolitan myths would then naturally be called the 'father of the gods'.

He was the third divine pharaoh and succeeded Shu to the throne. His reign also was disturbed. One text tells us how Geb caused the golden box

Papyrus of Tameniu showing the arched body of Nut, goddess of the sky, and Geb the earth-god with the 'Great Cackler', his emblem. Twenty-first Dynasty. British Museum.

Right: *The creation of the universe. The air-god, Shu, supports with his outstretched hands the body of Nut, the sky-goddess, while Geb, the god of the earth, lies at his feet.*

in which Ra's *uraeus* was kept to be opened in his presence. Ra had deposited the box, together with his cane and a lock of his hair, in a fortress on the eastern frontier of his empire as a potent and dangerous talisman. When opened, the breath of the divine serpent within killed all of Geb's companions then and there, and gravely burned Geb himself. Only the lock of Ra's hair, applied to the wound, could heal Geb. So great, indeed, was the virtue of this divine lock of hair that years later when it was plunged for purification into the lake of At Nub it immediately turned into a crocodile. When he was restored to health Geb administered his kingdom wisely and drew up a careful report on the condition of every province and town in Egypt.

Then he handed over his sovereignty to his eldest son, Osiris, and ascended to the heavens where at times he took the place of Thoth as Ra's herald and arbiter of the gods. Geb accompanied Ra on his journeys across the sky, acting as one of the crew of the solar barque. As Geb was one of the divine pharaohs and all the human pharaohs claimed to be descended from him, the royal throne was referred to in the *Pyramid Texts* as 'the throne of Geb'.

Nut

Nut, whom the Greeks sometimes identified with Rhea, was goddess of the sky, but it is debatable if in historical times she was the object of a genuine cult. She was Geb's twin sister and, it was said, married him secretly and against the will of Ra. Angered, Ra had the couple brutally separated by Shu and afterwards decreed that Nut could not bear a child in any given month of any year. Thoth, Plutarch tell us, happily had pity on her. Playing draughts with the Moon, he won in the course of several games a seventy-second part of the Moon's light, with which he composed five new days. As these five intercalated days did not belong to the official Egyptian calendar of three hundred and sixty days, Nut was thus able on the five days preceding the New Year to give birth successively to five children: Osiris, Haroeris (Horus), Set, Isis and Nephthys.

The sky-goddess is often represented as a woman with elongated body, touching the earth with toes and finger-tips, while her star-spangled belly is held aloft by Shu and forms the arch of the heavens. She also sometimes appears as a cow, for this is the form she assumed when, on the orders of Nun, she bore Ra on her back to the sky after Ra, as already related, decided to abandon his rebellious subjects. The dutiful cow rose obediently to her feet, rose higher and higher until she became dizzy and it was necessary to appoint a god to each of her four legs — which became the four pillars of the sky — in order to steady them. Shu, meanwhile, supported her belly, which became the firmament and to which Ra attached the stars and the constellations to light our earth. A variant of this story makes Nut a heavenly sow, whose belly was covered with little sucking pigs, the stars. Though she was often addressed by the title 'Daughter of Ra', she was also — in the legend which derived from her origin as a mother-goddess — called the mother of the sun, which was reborn in various fashions each morning from her womb. The rosy colour of the sky at dawn was supposed to be the blood which Nut shed in giving birth to the sun.

When she is pictured as a woman, Nut often wears a rounded vase on her head, this being the hieroglyph of her name. She is protectress of the dead, and we frequently see her holding the deceased close in her arms. On the inner lid of sarcophagi her starry body stretches above the mummy, watching maternally over him.

53

Osiris

Osiris, which is the Greek rendering of the Egyptian Usire, was identified by the Greeks with several of their own gods, but principally with Dionysus and Hades. At first Osiris was a nature god and embodied the spirit of vegetation which dies with the harvest to be reborn when the grain sprouts. Afterwards he was worshipped throughout Egypt as god of the dead and, in this capacity, became the most important god in the Egyptian pantheon.

Hieroglyphic texts contain numerous allusions to the life and deeds of Osiris during his sojourn on earth; but it is above all thanks to Plutarch that we know his legend so well.

The first son of Geb and Nut, Osiris was born in Thebes in Upper Egypt. At his birth a loud, mysterious voice proclaimed the coming of the 'Universal Lord', which gave rise to shouts of gladness, soon followed by tears and lamentations when it was learned what misfortunes awaited him. Ra rejoiced at the news of his birth in spite of the curse he had pronounced against Nut; and, having Osiris brought into his presence, he recognised his great-grandson as heir to his throne.

Osiris was handsome of countenance, dark-skinned and taller than all other men. When Geb, his father, retired to the heavens, Osiris succeeded him as king of Egypt and took Isis, his sister, as queen. The first care of the new sovereign was to abolish cannibalism and to teach his still half-savage subjects the art of fashioning agricultural implements. He taught them how to produce grain and grapes for man's nourishment in the form of bread, wine and beer. The cult of the gods did not yet exist, according to Heliopolitan belief, and Osiris instituted it. He built the first temples and sculpted the first divine images. He laid down the rules governing religious practice and even invented the two kinds of flute which should accompany ceremonial song. (The Memphite doctrine was, as has been said, that Ptah himself instituted religious practices and created the first images.)

After this he built towns and gave his people just laws, thus meriting the name Onnophris — 'the Good One' — by which, as the fourth divine pharaoh, he was known.

Not satisfied with having civilised Egypt, Osiris wished to spread the benefits of his rule throughout the whole world. He left the regency

Stela dedicated to the great Triad of Horus, Osiris and Isis, who appear in the upper panel, with two figures bearing offerings kneeling below. Osiris holds in his left hand the mystic 'vannus', emblem of majesty and dominion. The scribe Titiaa and his wife Aoui proffer gifts of fruit and flowers.

Right: *Limestone stela of Upuaut-mes, showing the deceased appearing before the gods Ra (right) and Osiris (left). c. 1300 B.C.*

to Isis and set forth on the conquest of Asia, accompanied by Thoth, his grand vizier, and his lieutenants Anubis and Upuaut. Osiris was the enemy of all violence, and it was by gentleness alone that he subjected country after country, winning and disarming their inhabitants by songs and the playing of various musical instruments. He returned to Egypt only after he had travelled the whole earth and spread civilisation everywhere. This part of the story bears such strong resemblances to the stories of Dionysus and Orpheus, that we may be entitled to wonder whether this is not an interpolation by Plutarch rather than the true Egyptian myth.

As Plutarch continued the story, Osiris found on his return to his kingdom that everything was in perfect order, for Isis had governed wisely in his absence. But it was not long before he became the victim of a plot organised by his brother Set, who was jealous of his power. Farther on we shall relate in detail how on the 17th Athyr, in the twenty-eighth year of his reign, Osiris 'the Good One' fell under the blows of the conspirators and how his faithful wife found his body and bore it

back to Egypt. Isis, thanks to her powers of sorcery and the aid of Thoth, Anubis and Horus, succeeded in bringing her husband's dead body back to life. Osiris soon answered Set's accusations and vindicated himself before the tribunal of gods, presided over by Geb.

Resurrected and thenceforward secure from the threat of death, Osiris could have regained his throne and continued to reign over the living. But he preferred to depart from this earth and retire to the 'Elysian Fields' where he warmly welcomed the souls of the just and reigned over the dead.

This was one version of the legend of Osiris. There seem, however, to have been many versions of the story. Perhaps more than in the case of any other god, the legend of Osiris underwent great changes through the course of history. In early times, certainly, he was a subsidiary god; some have even suggested that, except perhaps in the form related above, his myth did not originally belong to the systems of any of the great cosmogonies, but was subordinated at a late stage to the family of gods venerated at Heliopolis, Hermopolis, Memphis and Thebes, because the priests

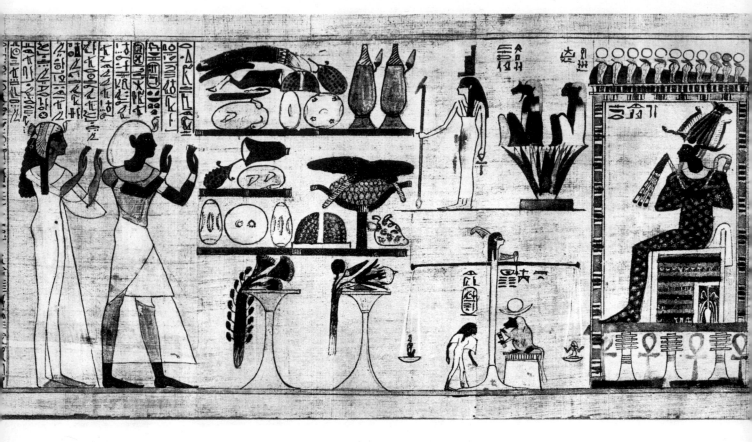

Papyrus of Queen Nejmet, who is seen with her husband before Osiris. In the lower panel the queen (right) is weighed in the scales against Mayet (left), the goddess of truth and justice.

of those centres were anxious that the Osiris cult should not entirely swamp their own. As Osiris in this powerful and universal form does not properly belong to the early Egyptian religious systems, we shall leave a full consideration of the cult to a later section.

It seems that the form of the Osiris myth related here may derive from the reign of a real king, for the name Usire means 'the seat of the Eye' and the Eye was the symbol of royal power in Egypt. The customary form of the legend is rather different and will be recounted when we discuss Isis and Set. It is a far more complicated myth and explains why Osiris became universalised as a god of the dead and how he was able to become so particularly associated with the well-being of the royal house.

Here, we shall only indicate briefly the many cosmic interpretations which the myth of Osiris was given.

As a vegetation spirit that dies and is ceaselessly reborn, Osiris represents the corn, the vine and the trees. He is also the Nile, which rises and falls every year; and the light of the sun, which vanishes in the shadows every evening to reappear more brilliantly at dawn. The struggle between the two brothers, Set and Osiris, is the war between the desert and the fertile earth, between the drying wind and the vegetation, between aridity and fecundity and between darkness and light.

But it was as god of the dead that Osiris enjoyed his greatest popularity: though he seems to have begun his mythic career as a rather frightening spirit of the Underworld, he ultimately came to represent for his devotees the hope of an eternally happy life in another world ruled over by a just and good king.

He was worshipped throughout Egypt in company with his wife Isis and Horus, his posthumous son, who formed with him a trinity. But he was particularly venerated at Abydos, where priests showed his tomb to the innumerable pilgrims who came to visit it. Happy were the favoured ones who were buried in the shadows of the august sanctuary, or who at least had a stela erected near by in their name to assure the benevolence of Osiris in after life!

Isis

Osiris is represented sometimes standing, sometimes seated on his throne, as a man tightly swathed in white mummy wrappings. His greenish face is surmounted by the high white mitre flanked by two ostrich feathers which is called 'Atef', the crown of Upper Egypt. Around his neck he wears a kind of cravat. His two hands, freed from the winding sheet, are folded across his breast and hold the whip and the sceptre in the form of a crook, emblems of supreme power.

The names and appellations of Osiris were countless. There are about a hundred in the litanies of *The Book of the Dead*.

Like many other gods, Osiris delighted in incarnations. He appeared not only in the form of various animals — the bull Onuphis, the sacred ram of Mendes, the bird Bennu (the phoenix) — but also in the 'Djed', a simple fetish which seems to have been his primitive form in the days when he led his prehistoric followers into battle. The 'Djed' was originally the trunk of a fir or some other conifer; but in classical times it was a kind of pillar with four capitals, which certain texts alleged to be the god's vertebral column.

Great festivals marked the critical dates in the Osiris legend. They were publicly celebrated, and in the course of the Mysteries then presented priests and priestesses would mime the passion and resurrection of the god.

Isis, mother of all things.

Isis (a Greek rendering of Aset or Eset) was identified by the Greeks with Demeter, Hera, Selene and even — because of a late confusion between Isis and Hathor — with Aphrodite. In later days the popularity of Isis became such that she finally absorbed the qualities of all the other goddesses; but originally she seems to have been a modest divinity of the Delta, the protective deity of Perehbet, north of Busiris, where she always retained a renowned temple.

Very soon she was given as wife to Osiris, the god of the neighbouring city, and indeed her name is thought by some to mean 'seat', in which case she would be interpreted as simply personifying the royal throne of Osiris. She bore him a son, Horus, who formed the third member of the trinity. Her popularity grew rapidly with that of her husband and son. This is her legend as Plutarch tells it to us:

The first daughter of Geb and Nut was born in the swamps of the Delta on the fourth intercalary day. Osiris, her eldest brother, chose her as his consort and she mounted to the throne with him. She helped him in his great work of civilising Egypt by teaching women to grind corn, spin flax and weave cloth. She also taught men the art of curing disease and, by instituting marriage, accustomed them to domestic life.

When her husband departed on his pacific conquest of the world she remained in Egypt as regent. She governed wisely while awaiting his return.

Isis was overwhelmed with grief at the news that Osiris had been assassinated by their brother, the violent Set. She cut off her hair, tore her robes and at once set forth in search of the coffer in which the good Osiris had been enclosed and which the conspirators had cast into the Nile.

This coffer had been carried out to sea by the waters of the Nile and borne across the waves to the Phoenician coast, where it came to rest at the base of a tamarisk tree. The tree grew with such astonishing rapidity that the chest was entirely enclosed within its trunk.

Now Malcandre, the King of Byblos, gave orders that the tamarisk should be cut down in order to serve as a prop for the roof of his palace. When this was done the marvellous tree gave off so exquisite a scent that its reputation reached the ears of Isis, who immediately understood its significance. Without delay she went to Phoenicia.

There the queen, Astarte, entrusted to her the care of her newly born son. Isis adopted the baby and would have conferred immortality upon it had its mother not broken the charm by her cries of terror upon seeing the goddess bathe the baby in purificatory flames. In order to reassure her, Isis revealed her true name and the reason for her presence. (This last episode bears such a strong resemblance to the legend of Demeter and Demophon in the Greek mythology that here again we must suspect Plutarch of embroidering on the original Egyptian myth.) Isis was, however, presented with the trunk of the miraculous tree. She drew forth the coffer containing her husband's body, bathed it in tears, and bore it back in haste to Egypt where, to deceive Set, she hid it in the swamps of Buto. Set, however, regained possession of his brother's body by chance and in order to annihilate it for ever cut it into fourteen pieces and scattered them far and wide.

Isis, undiscouraged, began a patient search for the precious fragments and found them all except the phallus, which had been greedily devoured by a Nile crab, the Oxyrhynchid, for ever accursed for this crime.

The goddess reconstituted the body of Osiris, cunningly joining the fragments together. She then performed, for the first time in history, the rites of embalmment, and this restored the murdered god to eternal life. It was always considered in Egypt that eternal life for the soul depended on the preservation intact of the physical body. In early days the drying effects of wind and sand were relied upon to preserve the body; but under the spreading influence of the Osiris cult, embalmment came to be employed. In performing the rites of embalmment, Isis was assisted by her sister Nephthys (though she was Set's wife), by her nephew Anubis, by Osiris' grand vizier Thoth and (rather inconsistently) by Horus, the posthumous son, conceived by union with her husband's dead body, miraculously reanimated by her charms.

A Nubian relief of Isis. Daughter of Geb and Nut, sister and wife of Osiris, she is also the mother of Horus and, with Nephthys, divine mourner.

Right: *Detail from the figure of Hathor, as a cow, giving milk to the young Amenhotep II.*

Afterwards Isis retired to the swamps of Buto to escape the wrath of Set, who now occupied the throne, and to bring up her son Horus until the day when he should be of an age to avenge his father. According to another version, Set imprisoned Isis; but with the aid of Thoth, she managed to escape and so hide from Set the fact that she had conceived a child. She took refuge in the swamps and there gave birth to Horus. But she had no means of support for herself and the child, and was therefore forced to go out begging. One day, when she had been out all day, leaving the baby Horus hidden in the reeds, she came back to find him writhing about and half dead. Set, who was unable to enter the marshes in his real form, had taken the form of a poisonous snake and had

The chief festival associated with the cult of Isis (above) was held at Busiris and, according to Herodotus, was an elaborate celebration.

Left: *A relief from one of the storage chambers in the Great Temple at Abu Simbel.*

crept up on Horus and bitten him. Isis was in despair, seemingly alone in the world: her father, her mother and her elder brother (Osiris) were dead; her younger brother (Set) was her implacable enemy and her sister Nephthys was his wife. Isis therefore appealed to all mankind. The marsh-dwellers and fishermen immediately came to offer their help and they wept in sympathy, but none of them knew a magical spell which would cure Horus of this poison. Isis guessed that the cause of the evil was Set: his poisoning assumed cosmic proportions, representing the danger that the embodiment of innocence and son of goodness may be destroyed by the principle of evil and cunning.

This is the earliest manifestation of the great struggle between Horus and Set, which we shall meet again in the story of Horus. Isis now calls upon the high god for aid. Her plea is heard in the 'Boat of Millions of Years', which when it draws level with her interrupts its course. Thoth descends from the boat to speak with Isis and, after expressing surprise that with her magic powers Isis is unable to set matters right, assures her that the power of Ra is at her disposal. When the sun's boat stops the light stops with it, and Thoth tells Isis that the darkness will persist until Horus is cured. Isis can hardly believe that Thoth is able on behalf of Ra to put things right, but she and Thoth realise the significance of the sun's stopping until Horus is cured: it means that if Horus dies, Ra's whole creation (i.e. the world) will be annihilated and Set, the principle of evil, will reign supreme. And Isis wishes that she were Horus herself, so that she should not have to see the consequences of his death. Thoth, however, reassures her, declaring that the magical protection enjoyed by Horus will henceforward be equal to that of the sun. Then, in the name of the sun, Thoth exorcises the poison from Horus' body, saying that the boat of Ra will stand still, that there will be no food, that the temples will be closed, that misery will never depart from the world, that eternal darkness will reign, that the wells will be dry, that their will be no crops and no vegetation until Horus is cured. This powerful spell of the sun-god Ra conquers the poison, and Isis and all the marsh-dwellers rejoice. Thoth then recommends the child to their care, saying that he is now their responsibility on earth. Ra and Osiris will watch over him and Isis will spread his cult, and make him loved and respected. Finally, Thoth reports his success to Ra, saying that his *son* Horus has been saved.

This story, which touched the Egyptians deeply for its pathos, was also symbolic of the relation of the pharaoh to Ra and to the people. Horus being considered the archetype of the pharaohs, the message of the story seems to be that Ra is supremely concerned with the welfare of his 'son', the pharaoh, and is able to protect him against all attacks by his enemies; but that it is also the duty of the people to love and respect the pharaoh and, as far as they can, to protect him. If the pharaoh should come to harm, the whole world order would collapse and the people themselves would necessarily die.

Against every other peril which assailed Horus while he lay hidden in the marshes of the Delta Isis was able to protect him. For she was a potent magician and even the gods were not immune from her sorcery. It was told how, when she was still only a simple woman in the service of Ra, she persuaded the great god to confide to her his secret name. Connected in the Egyptian mind with beliefs in magic incantations or spells was the belief that the knowledge of a person's name gave one power over that person — either because it revealed the key to his identity (indeed the person was inseparable from the name) or because it made it possible to recite spells against the person. Isis took advantage of the fact that the sun-god was now an old man with shaking head and dribbling mouth. With earth moistened with the divine spittle she fashioned a venomous snake which bit Ra cruelly. Ra was incapable of curing himself of a wound whose origin he did not understand, and moaning with pain called all the gods to his side. But none of Ra's children could help him — they could only bewail his lot. Isis now approached him, seemingly innocent and asked him solicitously what had happened. 'Has a snake poisoned you? Can it be that one of your own creatures has turned to strike at you? I shall conquer it with my spells! I shall make it recoil at the sight of your majesty!' Then Ra explained how he had been attacked by a serpent as he was making his usual daily journey, and told Isis what fearful pain he was in. 'It is not fire; it is not water. For I am colder than water and I am hotter than fire, and all my body sweats. My eye trembles so that I cannot see the sky.' Isis replied, 'Tell me your name, divine father, for

a man lives when his name is pronounced'. So Ra answered: 'I am the creator of the earth and of the mountains and of all that is upon the earth. I made the water and I made the sky and I placed the soul of the gods therein. When I open my eyes daylight appears, and when I shut them the night falls. At my command the mysterious waters of the Nile burst forth. I created the hours and the days. I give the signal for the festivals of the year and make the river. I am Khepri in the morning, Ra at midday and Atum in the evening.' But this did not cure Ra, for he still had not told his secret name. Isis insisted that she could do nothing until he confided his real name. As soon as he told her this she would be able to cure him. At last Ra realised that there was no alternative but to give in to Isis. Therefore, hiding himself from the other gods, he caused the secret name to pass directly from his own bosom into that of Isis, at the same time forbidding her to reveal it to anyone other than her son Horus. We may see in this myth, as in the myth of Isis and Horus in the marshes, an attempt to illustrate how the supreme power was transmitted to the Osirian triad, in particular how the sun's power was communicated to Horus, or to his earthly counterpart, the pharaoh.

Isis, in the Osirian myth, represents the rich plains of Egypt, made fruitful by the annual inundation of the Nile which is Osiris, who is separated from her by Set, the arid desert.

Her cult continued to grow in importance until it ultimately absorbed that of nearly all other goddesses. Though with the expansion of the Osiris cult, a frequent representation of Isis is as a mourner over a mummy (and we have seen in the legend of the marshes that one of her essential functions was to spread the worship of the Osirian triad), with her husband, she increasingly entered the realm of the living and was more widely worshipped as a fertility-goddess. Ultimately the names of Nut, Hathor and Isis became interchangeable as mother-goddesses.

In the Nile valley Isis kept her worshippers until well into Christian times. It was not until the middle of the sixth century, in the reign of

Right: *The serpent, Apep, Ra's eternal foe, was a malevolent figure and an enemy of the dead. Here the deceased, with the help of his three sons (shown in the lower panel), endeavours to placate him. British Museum.*

Justinian, that the temple of Philae — her chief sanctuary in the extreme south of the country — was closed to her cult and turned into a church.

Great festivals were celebrated in spring and autumn in honour of Isis. The splendours of the processions which then took place have been described to us by Apuleius, who was an initiate in the mysteries of Isis. Thanks to him we can raise a corner of the veil which conceals the secret ceremonies of initiation.

Isis is normally represented as a woman who bears on her head a throne, the hieroglyph of her name. Occasionally, but later, her head-dress is a disk, set between cow's horns, sometimes flanked with two feathers. Finally, we sometimes find her represented with a cow's head set on a human body. These horns and the cow's head merely prove that by then Isis was identified with Hathor; but Plutarch, though he says he does not believe it, gives us another explanation. Isis, he tells us,

wished to intervene on behalf of Set who, though her husband's murderer, was also her own brother. She tried to cheat her son Horus of his just vengeance; but Horus turned in rage against his mother and cut off her head. Thoth then transformed it by enchantment and gave her the head of a cow.

The cow is, on the other hand, the animal sacred to Isis, who also possessed as fetishes the magic knot 'Tat', called 'the Knot of Isis', and the sistrum, the emblem of Hathor.

Sculpture and painting often represent her beside Osiris, whom she helps or protects — as she does the dead — with her winged arms. She may be seen mourning at the foot of sarcophagi or watching over Canopic jars in the form of a kite, and she is then often accompanied by Nephthys in the same guise. Isis also frequently appears in the role of mother, suckling the infant Horus or joining him in his struggles against Set.

Set

Set (or Seth or Sutekh), whom the Greeks called Typhon, was the name of Osiris' wicked brother who finally became the incarnation of the spirit of evil, in eternal opposition to the spirit of good.

The son of Geb and Nut, he was, Plutarch tells us, prematurely born on the third intercalary day. He tore himself violently from his mother's womb. He was rough and wild, his skin was white and his hair was red — an abomination to the Egyptians, who compared it to the pelt of an ass.

Set was jealous of Osiris, his elder brother, and secretly aspired to the throne. In order to seize it he availed himself of the great festivals which were celebrated at Memphis on the occasion of Osiris' victorious return to his kingdom. Having first assured himself of the presence of seventy-two accomplices, he invited his brother to a banquet during the course of which he gave orders that a marvellously fashioned coffer should be brought in. This chest, he explained as if in jest, would belong to whomsoever it fitted exactly. Osiris, falling in with the pleasantry, lay down in the coffer without suspicion. The conspirators at once rushed forward, closed the lid and nailed it firmly down. They threw it into the Nile, whence it was carried to the sea and across to Byblos. We have already seen how Isis brought it back to Egypt and how Set, hunting by moonlight in the swamps of the Delta, found it again by chance, and how, when he had recognised his brother's corpse, he cut it up into fourteen pieces which he either cast into the Nile, or scattered far and wide through Egypt. This time the usurper felt that his possession of the realm was assured, and it worried him little that his wife Nephthys had left him. Nephthys, indeed, had joined the party of Osiris as most of the other gods had done, escaping from the cruelties of the tyrant by taking refuge in the bodies of various animals. Meanwhile Horus, son of Isis, was growing to maturity in the shelter of the Delta swamps, and we shall see how he avenged the murder of Osiris, his father, and reclaimed his heritage from Set.

Set, in Osirian myth, figures as the eternal adversary, a personification of the arid desert, of drought and darkness in opposition to the fertile earth, life-bringing water and light. All that is creation and blessing comes from Osiris; all that is destruction and perversity arises from Set.

In primitive times, however, the evil character of Set was not so accentuated. The old *Pyramid Texts* make him not the brother of Osiris, but the brother of Horus the Elder, and speak of terrible struggles between them which were terminated by the judgment of the gods, who proclaimed Horus the victor and banished Set to the desert. It was said that his life was spared only on condition that, as god of the wind, he should provide a gentle breeze to bear along the boat of Osiris.

It was only later, when the Osirian myth had grown and when the two Horuses had become confused, that Set was made the uncle of Horus and the eternal enemy of Osiris.

Originally Set seems to have been the Lord of Upper Egypt, who was overthrown by the worshippers of the falcon god. The legendary struggles between the brother gods may thus reflect historical events.

The bas-reliefs of the Old and the Middle Kingdoms show Set and Horus together leading prisoners to the king, or else together at the base of the royal throne binding the plants of Upper and Lower Egypt around the emblem which expresses the idea of union — thus making the symbolic gesture of *sam-taui*, the union of the two countries.

A function which Set no doubt preserved from

Horus and Set (with the head of the Typhonian Animal) symbolise the union of the two Egypts by binding together heraldic plants of North and South. Bas-relief from tablet of Sesostris I. Twelfth Dynasty.

his earlier character in the tradition of the solar myths was that of one of the crew of the solar barque. He was one of those who stood in the boat during its journey in order to defend Ra against his enemies. Set, being a warlike god, traditionally defended Ra against his most implacable and dangerous foe, the serpent Apep or Apophis. In the trial to decide between Horus and Set, Set boasts of his prowess in daily defending Ra, and claims that on account of his great strength he should be awarded the kingdom. But *The Book of the Dead* describes how Set is not content merely to have the honour of defending the chief of the gods. There is more braggadocio about him than real courage, and having slain Apep, partly by ruse, he then turns to Ra to proclaim his triumph and to demand that Ra should recognise how brave he is. He says tauntingly to Ra that he can come out of hiding now that Apep is dead, bringing with him all his paraphernalia (i.e. his divine symbols of supreme power). Finally he warns Ra to treat him well or he will raise his storms and thunder against him. (Even at this stage Set was a storm-god and god of the winds, if not yet the personification of destructive forces.) At this Ra orders his

The terrace temple of Queen Hatshepsut built at Deir el Bahri in the Theban necropolis at the beginning of the Eighteenth Dynasty at the side of an old temple of the Eleventh Dynasty.

crew to chase Set away, which they do, Nut calling Set a windbag, and Ra makes his divine dawn appearance. As can be seen, this myth combines the two aspects of Set. His presence in his good aspect as the slayer of Apep is essential to the safe passage of Ra on his daily voyage; but it is equally essential that he should be banished from the boat before the divine party can proceed. The last requirement no doubt explains why Set was rarely depicted in representations of the solar barque.

Under the domination of the Hyksos, the new rulers identified Set with their own great warrior god Sutekh and had a temple built for him in Avaris, their capital. Under the New Empire, Rameses II, whose father was named Seti, the 'Setian', did not hesitate to proclaim himself the 'Beloved of Set'. The worshippers of Osiris, however, were indignant that a cult should be rendered to the murderer of the 'Good One', and Seti caused the cursed image to be effaced from the engraved tablets on the walls of his tomb and proclaimed himself no longer the 'Setian', but the 'Osirian'.

It is only towards the middle of the tenth century, under the kings of the Twenty-second Dynasty, that the assassin of Osiris really began to undergo the punishment for his crime. His statues were broken and on the bas-reliefs his features were smashed with hammers. Anyone who wrote his name was forced to erase it. Finally he was driven from the Egyptian pantheon and made a god of the unclean. Set, the ancient Lord of Upper Egypt, ended by becoming a kind of devil, enemy of all the gods.

Asses, antelopes and other desert animals were supposed to belong to Set, and also the hippopotamus, the boar, the crocodile and the scorpion, in whose bodies the god of evil and his partisans had sought refuge from the blows of the conquering Horus. Legend says that Set, in the guise of a black pig, had once wounded Horus in the eye. In the same form each month he attacked and devoured the moon where, according to some, the soul of Osiris had taken refuge.

Set is represented as having the features of a fantastic beast with a thin, curved snout, straight, square-cut ears and a stiff forked tail. This creature cannot with certainty be identified and is commonly called the 'Typhonian Animal'. Sometimes Set is depicted as a man with the head of this strange quadruped.

65

Nephthys

Nephthys is the Greek rendering of Nebthet, and is called by Plutarch Aphrodite and Nike.

She is pictured as a woman wearing on her head the two hieroglyphs with which her name, which signifies 'Mistress of the Palace', was written: i.e. a basket (neb) placed on the sign for palace (het). It is thought that her name may betoken that she is a personification of Osiris' residence. In origin a goddess of the dead, Nephthys in the Osirian legend becomes the second daughter of Geb and Nut. Set, her second brother, took her for his wife, but she remained barren. She wanted a child by her eldest brother Osiris and with this object she made him drunk and drew him into her arms without his being aware of it. The fruit of this union was Anubis.

Nephthys, according to this legend, seems to represent the desert's edge, ordinarily arid but sometimes fruitful when the Nile floods are especially high. When Set committed fratricide his wife abandoned him in horror and, joining the party of Osiris' defenders, she helped her sister Isis to embalm the corpse of the murdered god, alternating with her in the funerary lamentations. A papyrus still preserves for us the text.

Just as Nephthys and Isis had protected the mummy of their brother, so the 'twins', as the kites perched at either end of funeral beds are often called, also watched over the bodies of the dead men who, by virtue of the funeral rites, had become 'Osirises'. On coffin-lids and the walls of sarcophagi we often see them represented, standing or kneeling, stretching forth their long, winged arms in a gesture of protection.

Horus

Horus is the Latin rendering of the Greek Hores and the Egyptian Hor. He was a solar god constantly identified with Apollo and represented by a falcon or a falcon-headed god.

Under the name Hor — which in Egyptian sounds like a word meaning 'sky' — the Egyptians referred to the falcon which they saw soaring high above their heads, and many thought of the sky as a divine falcon whose two eyes were the sun and the moon. The worshippers of this bird must have been numerous and powerful; for it was carried as a totem on prehistoric standards and from the earliest times was considered the pre-eminent divine being. Consideration of his pre-eminence led to the belief in Upper Egypt that the king was his earthly embodiment. This belief later hardened into dogma and the kings took the name of Horus as one of their own. The hieroglyph which represents the idea of 'god' was a falcon on its perch.

Wherever the followers of the falcon settled, Horus was worshipped; but in the course of time and in the different sanctuaries which were dedicated to him his role and attributes varied. Thus we find in the Egyptian pantheon some twenty Horuses, among whom it is important to distinguish Horus the Elder, 'Haroeris', and other falcons of a solar character such as Hor Behdetite, Horus of Edfu, from Horus, son of Isis, of the Osirian legend — i.e., 'Harsiesis', the infant avenger of his father. As we have already remarked, the Egyptians of the later periods were themselves to confuse the solar Horus and the Osirian god of the same name.

Bas-relief with scarab and Horus figures, from the tomb of Seti I.

The temple of Horus at Edfu. There seems to be a connection between Horus, the great sun-god, and the god Hat or Har-Hat, a good genius who protected the persons of kings and the temples of the gods.

Haroeris is the Greek rendering of Har Wer, which means Horus the Great, or Horus the Elder.

He was worshipped at Letopolis under the title Horkhenti Irti, 'Horus who rules the two eyes', and at Pharboethos under the name Hor Merti, 'Horus of the two eyes'. He is the god of the sky itself and his two eyes are the sun and the moon, whose birth, according to Herodotus, was celebrated on the last day of Epiphi, when these two astral bodies are in conjunction.

In the *Pyramid Texts* Haroeris is the son of Ra and brother of Set, and the eternal struggle between darkness and light is symbolised by the endless battles in which Set tears out the eye of Horus while Horus castrates his implacable enemy. In the early texts the Horus of this legend was Horus the Elder, but later sources make the great epic battle take place between Set and Horus, the son of Osiris. In either version, however, the tribunal of the gods gave judgment in favour of Horus, who from the end of the Second Dynasty was considered to be the divine ancestor of the pharaohs, in whose records he is given the title Hor Nubti: 'Horus the Vanquisher of Set'.

Harakhtes is the Greek rendering of Harakhte and means 'Horus of the Horizon'. He represents the sun on its daily course between the eastern and western horizon. Early confused with Ra, he successively usurped all of Ra's roles, until Ra, in his turn, assumed all of Horus' epithets and became pre-eminent throughout Egypt under the name Ra-Harakhte.

Column with relief of King Thuthmosis IV, wearing a warrior's crown and carrying lotus flowers. Above his head hovers a Horus falcon, the pharaohs' protective divinity. Eighteenth Dynasty.

68

Behdety, 'He of Behdet' (or Hor Behdetite) is another name of the great celestial Horus. He was worshipped at Behdet, a district of ancient Edfu. The Greeks called it Apollinopolis Magna and recognised Apollo as Lord of the sanctuary. The Egyptians explained the connection of Horus with Edfu as follows:

In the reign of Ra-Harakhte as king of Upper and Lower Egypt the royal army was in Nubia when the King — who is referred to not as the sun-god but as an earthly ruler — was informed that there was a plot against him in Egypt. The plotters seem to have been some kind of demons and, as we shall see, their leader was Set. The King sailed downstream and, landing at Edfu, ordered his son Horus to fight the enemy. Horus flew up into the sky, taking the form of a winged sun-disk and, seeing the enemy, flew down to attack them. He inflicted such damage on them that they fled. As a reward for his prowess, the King, when he heard of this rout, awarded his son the title Horus Behdety, or Horus of Edfu.

The enemy were, however, not yet defeated, for they changed themselves into crocodiles and

Section of a symbolic tableau depicting the course of the sun. Four minor divinities with scarab and serpent heads bear Ra-Harakhte, the sun-god, in triumph. New Kingdom. Bibliothèque Nationale.

69

hippopotami and attacked the boat of Ra-Harakhte himself. Again, Horus and his followers routed them by harpooning them from the boat. Once more assuming the form of a winged sun-disk and setting himself at the prow of the boat, Horus pursued the survivors throughout Upper and Lower Egypt inflicting terrible defeats upon them.

In the second part of this story, the characters change somewhat, for Horus, son of Ra, becomes confused with Horus, son of Osiris. The leader of the enemy is now Set, the enemy of Osiris. Set takes the form of a serpent and the fighting continues throughout Lower Egypt as far as the frontiers of Asia. Horus is, however, victorious. To seal his victory, he again sails upstream to Upper Egypt and puts down another rebellion. As a reward for this triumph, Ra-Harakhte decrees that the winged sun-disk should be placed on all temples and shrines of all deities in order to ward off enemies.

Behdety is usually represented in the form of a winged sun-disk; and his followers liked to sculpt his image above temple gates. He often appears in battle scenes hovering above the pharaoh like a great falcon with outspread wings — his original form — clutching in its claws the mystic fly-whisk and the ring, symbolic of eternity.

The bas-reliefs in the temple of Edfu portray him as a falcon-headed god leading into battle against Set the armies of Ra-Harakhte, who himself embodied in a single deity the union of Ra and a special form of Horus worshipped at Heliopolis.

Harmakhis is the Greek rendering of Hor-makhet, which means 'Horus who is on the Horizon'. The name has often been wrongly employed in the form of Ra-Harmakhis for Ra-Harakhte. It is the proper name of the huge sphinx sixty feet high and more than a hundred and eighty feet long sculpted nearly five thousand years ago in the image of King Khephren in a rock near the pyramid which it guards. He is a personification of the rising sun and a symbol (for the comfort of Khephren) of resurrection.

An early mother and child theme in religion: Isis and the infant Horus. She wears on her head a disk set between the horns of a cow, representing the sistrum, a musical instrument usually carried by Hathor.

Raised on the edge of the desert, even its colossal size did not in ancient days protect it against the invading sands. A stela tells us how it appeared in a dream to the future Thuthmosis IV. Thuthmosis was at the time a simple royal prince and not heir to the throne. While hunting he fell asleep in the shadow of the sphinx and dreamed that it spoke to him, ordering him to remove the covering sand and promising in return to heap favours upon him. 'Oh my son Thuthmosis,' it cried, 'it is I, thy father, Harmakhis-Khepri-Atum. The throne will be thine . . . so that thou shalt do what my heart desires . . .'

Harsiesis is the Greek rendering of Hor-sa-iset i.e. 'Horus, the son of Isis'. We have already seen how Isis was reputed to have conceived Horus by her husband Osiris, but after his death, and how the popularity of mother and son continued to increase, together with that of Osiris himself. This popularity became such that Harsiesis — originally a minor falcon-god from the neighbourhood of Buto, who was called Horus the Younger in order to distinguish him from the great sky-god Horus the Elder — ended by eclipsing all the other Horuses whose roles and attributes he successively took over.

The Osirian legend recounts the posthumous birth of the child which Isis had of Osiris by magical means, reanimating the corpse of the murdered god. It relates how she gave premature birth to Horus on the floating island of Chemmis in the marshes not far from Buto. In early youth he was frequently called 'the infant Horus' — Harpakhrad — or Harpokrates. Harpokrates is represented as a baby, nude or adorned only with jewellery. His head is shaved, except for the sidelock of youth which falls over his temple. Often he is seated on his mother's lap while she offers him her breast. He sucks his thumb like a baby, a gesture which was misinterpreted by the Greeks, who took it for a symbol of discretion, and won the young god fame as the divinity of silence.

For fear of the machinations of Set, Horus was brought up in seclusion. He was extremely weak at birth and escaped from the numerous dangers which menaced him only by his mother's power of sorcery. The memory of these sufferings is preserved for us in the magic formulas which were employed by sorcerers to cure patients similarly afflicted.

The child Horus grew, and Osiris appeared frequently to him and instructed him in the use of arms so that he should soon be able to make war on Set, reclaim his inheritance and avenge his father. This glorious action was to earn for Horus the epithet Harendotes, which is the Greek for Har-end-yotef, 'Horus protector of his father'.

The campaigns of the young god against the murderer of Osiris are sculpted on the walls of the temple at Edfu, whose great god Behdety was, in this later epoch, identified with Harsiesis, while Set was confused with Apep, the eternal enemy of the sun (though, as we have seen, Set was in fact the slayer of Apep). In a long series of bas-reliefs we see Horus, under the name Hartomes, 'Horus the Lancer', piercing his adversaries with his lance. Meanwhile Horus' followers cut Set's followers into pieces — though they vainly attempt to seek refuge in the bodies of crocodiles, hippopotami, antelopes and so forth.

The war drags on, and Set attempts to terminate it through arbitration by a tribunal of the gods. First he has Osiris summoned before it; but Osiris is so well defended by Thoth that the gods declare in favour of Osiris, who is found to be 'true of voice'. Set, however, cannot accept that Horus should ascend the throne, and has him too brought before the court. This trial is the subject of one of the few consecutive stories connected with the Egyptian mythology that have survived. The court cannot make a decision either way, for its members, presided over by Ra-Harakhte, seem always to agree with the last speaker brought to testify before them, and they constantly change their minds. After the trial has already lasted for eighty years, they are all heartily bored with it and totally unable to resolve their differences. Most of the tribunal favour Horus, who against Set's accusations that his nephew is a bastard, only the alleged son of Osiris, has established the legitimacy of his birth; but the president, Ra-Harakhte, favours Set because he is the son of Nut.

Though he has fought a lengthy war with Set and has been before the tribunal for eighty years, Horus is still represented as little more than a child. Set, according to Ra-Harakhte, is the older and more experienced and therefore the better fitted to be the ruler of Egypt; Horus, who claims the throne by right of succession, is too young to govern. In symbolic terms, therefore, the great struggle between Horus and Set represents conflicting opinions about what reasons a man may adduce in claiming rights over property. While Horus claims by right of succession, Set boasts that he is the strongest in the great Ennead (i.e. stronger than Ra himself), for every day he kills Apep, the chief enemy of the sun-god. Horus has no defence but the law of succession and the justice of the gods.

The story opens after eighty years of wrangling with Shu and Thoth recommending Horus' case to the tribunal on the grounds that justice should prevail over brute strength. Isis immediately thinks that the issue is settled and Shu declares that the will of the tribunal is that the Eye (symbol of royal power) should be presented to Horus. But Ra-Harakhte is offended that the conduct of the tribunal has been snatched away from him in this way and, furious, stops the gods from presenting the Eye to Horus. Set suggests trial by combat; but Thoth opposes this on the grounds that it would be to avoid the vital decision as to who was in the right. The tribunal is once more in deadlock. They decide to summon the ram-god of Mendes, who comes before them together with Ptah of the primeval mound. But neither of them is prepared to give judgment, merely suggesting that the tribunal should write for guidance to Neith, the goddess of Sais, the oldest of the goddesses. Thoth is instructed to write a formal letter requesting her views. Neith, like the other gods, favours Horus. She replies that the throne should be given to Horus, while Set should receive compensation in the form of twice his existing property and two more wives, Astarte and Anat, who were Syrian goddesses. The gods of the tribunal once more think that a solution has at last been reached and cry out that Neith is right. Once more, however, Ra-Harakhte resents their haste, and reproaches Horus with his youth. Tempers among the gods are by now short and, seeing that only Ra-Harakhte's obstinacy is keeping them, Baba calls out to him: 'Your shrine is empty'.

Mortally offended at this insult, Ra lies down on his back and sulks. The tribunal breaks up. Only Hathor is able to persuade him to rejoin the tribunal; going to her father's house, she shows him her private parts, and so cheers him up that he forgets his displeasure!

Reconvened, argument in the tribunal again hinges on the two methods of inheritance: by

Bronze figure of Harpokrates, 'the child Horus', here seen wearing the double crown or pschent of the South and the North. Usually represented as an infant with his finger to his lips.

ability or by patrilineal succession. As each case is put the gods applaud it and they get no further.

Now Isis, whom Set has had excluded from the tribunal, bribes Anty to ferry her over to the Middle Island, to which the court has shifted. Always a powerful sorceress, Isis then transforms herself into a ravishing young maiden; Set sees her from where he is seated with the other gods and goes secretly over to waylay her. When he speaks to her she tells him a story of how her husband, a shepherd, has died leaving her with a little boy who looks after his father's cattle; of how a stranger came up to the son and said: 'I shall beat you, take your father's cattle and chase you away'. Isis then asks Set if he will help her son against this stranger. Set, hoping to please the beautiful maiden, answers: 'Should cattle be given to strangers when a man has a son as heir?' Thereupon Isis transforms herself into a kite, flies up to the top of a tree, and calls down to Set that he has condemned himself out of his own mouth.

Set, overwhelmed at the injustice of this trickery, goes weeping to complain to Ra. But Ra can only agree with Isis, that Set has condemned himself.

Ra now becomes impatient to end the dispute and instructs the gods, who have sat down idly on a mountainside, that they should immediately place the crown on Horus' head. But Set will not accept this judgment. He proposes, and the gods agree, that he and Horus should decide the issue by both turning themselves into hippopotami and diving into the water. Whichever of the two comes out of the water before the end of three months should be declared the loser. Isis is in despair, for she is sure that Set intends to kill Horus. So she takes a harpoon on a length of rope and casts it into the water. It first pierces Horus, who cries out to her to order the harpoon to release him, and this she does. When she next casts the harpoon into the water it catches Set, who cries out to her to release him likewise, appealing to her as his sister and in memory of their common mother. Isis is too sentimental not to listen to this plea and releases him. Horus, furious at this, comes out of the water and cuts his mother's head off. The gods resolve to punish him for this crime, but cannot find him, for he has gone into hiding on a mountain. Set, however, is able to find Horus, and tears out his eyes,

burying them on the mountain. Lotus flowers, symbol of rebirth and of the sun, grow out of the eyes. Set returns to the gods and tells them that he cannot find Horus. But Hathor, or sometimes Thoth, finds him lying on the mountainside and rubs milk into his eye sockets. Horus opens his eyes and finds that they have been restored and returns to the company of the gods with Hathor.

The struggle is renewed and every weapon is used: calumny, sexual insults, trickery and force. A decision still cannot be reached. Neith is again approached, but again without success. Finally, and decisively, it is decided on the advice of Thoth to appeal to Osiris for final judgment.

Osiris naturally replies in favour of his son, reproaching the gods for delaying the judgment for so long and for ill-treating Horus. Was Osiris not the god whom they had to thank for their barley and spelt and cattle? No other god performed such services. Ra, angered at this, retorts that even if Osiris had never existed there would still be barley and spelt.

Osiris' reply to this curt letter settles the dispute, and defines the spheres of power of the god of the living and the god of the dead. Osiris praises the supreme god of the Ennead for all that he has done, including the establishment of the halls of judgment in the Underworld. But Osiris does not veil his threat. He speaks of the 'savage-faced messengers' he has at his disposal, whom he can send to fetch the heart of any god or mortal who performs evil deeds. It is ordained that every being — gods and stars, nobles and common people — shall pass into the West, the land of the dead. There they shall be subject to the judgment of Osiris, who is thus ultimately the lord of all of them.

Backed by this threat, the judgment of Osiris in favour of his son is accepted by the tribunal. Set's pride, however, still does not allow him to accept legal judgment rather than judgment through force of arms. He is brought in chains before the gods, who spare his life on condition that, as god of storms and the wind, he will convey the boat of Osiris.

Horus' heritage is now restored to him and he is declared ruler of the two Egypts. He thus earns two further titles: Harsomtus or Heru-Sam-Taui ('Horus who united the two countries') and Harpa-neb-taui ('Horus Lord of the two lands').

Horus re-established everywhere the authority of Osiris and the solar cycle. He erected temples in which he was represented in the various forms he had assumed during the wars against his irreconcilable enemies, the followers of Set. He then reigned peacefully over Egypt, of which he always remained the national god, ancestor of the pharaohs, who each took the title of 'the Living Horus'.

With his father Osiris and his mother Isis, Horus was worshipped throughout Egypt. He figures in the triads or trinities of numerous sanctuaries, either as chief, as prince consort, or as divine infant. Thus at Edfu and at Ombos he is the great god with Hathor as his companion; while Hathor is the uncontested mistress at Dendera, and Horus, in his role of the sovereign's husband, only a privileged guest.

Until the beginning of the New Kingdom, temple figures represent Horus acting in consort with Set to crown and purify the king. They show the king into the sanctuary or perform the symbolic gesture of *sam-taui*. But later Thoth everywhere replaces Set. Elsewhere we see Horus fighting Set and his partisans, mourning Osiris and performing for him the burial duties. Finally in the next world Horus ushers the deceased into the presence of 'the Good One' and often presides over the weighing of his soul.

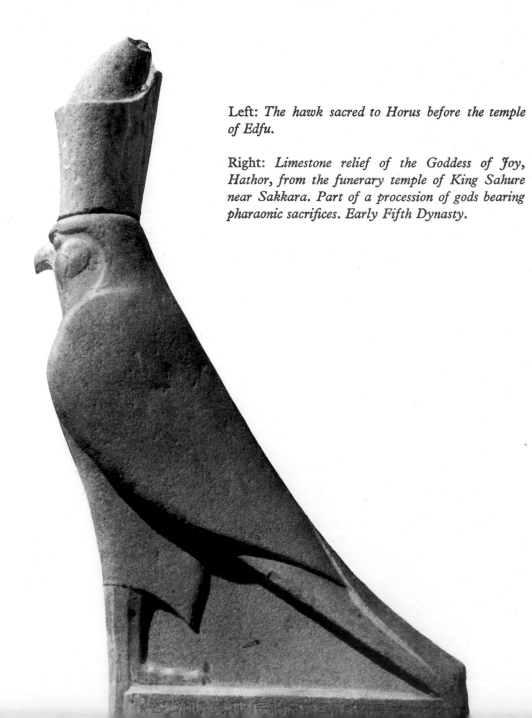

Left: *The hawk sacred to Horus before the temple of Edfu.*

Right: *Limestone relief of the Goddess of Joy, Hathor, from the funerary temple of King Sahure near Sakkara. Part of a procession of gods bearing pharaonic sacrifices. Early Fifth Dynasty.*

Hathor

Hathor (Athyr) is the name of the great Egyptian deity whom the Greeks identified with Aphrodite.

A sky-goddess, she was originally described as the daughter of Ra and the wife of Horus. She was, however, sometimes called the mother of Horus; for her name can be interpreted as meaning 'the dwelling of Horus' and it was explained that within her the sun-god resided, being enclosed each evening in her breast, to be born again each morning.

The texts also say that she was the great celestial cow who created the world and all that it contains, including the sun.

She is in consequence represented as a cow — her sacred animal — or as a cow-headed goddess. Still more often she is given a human head adorned either with horns or simply a cow's ears and heavy tresses framing her face.

Hathor also had a fetish in which she liked to embody herself: the sistrum, a musical instrument which drove away evil spirits. It was in a spirit of piety that the architect of Dendera conceived the columns of Hathor's temple as so many colossal sistra.

Hathor was the protectress of women and was supposed to preside at their toilet. She enjoyed immense popularity as the goddess of joy and love. She was proclaimed mistress of merriment and sovereign of the dance, mistress of music and sovereign of song, of leaping and jumping and the weaving of garlands. Her temple was the 'home of intoxication and a place of enjoyment'.

Hathor nourished the living with her milk. We see her giving her breast to the king whom she holds in her arms or on her knees and, again, in the form of a cow, suckling the pharaoh.

Although she was well disposed towards those who were alive she cherished the dead even more tenderly. Under the name 'Queen of the West' she was the protectress of the Theban necropolis. Vignettes in *The Book of the Dead* show the good cow half-emerged from the Libyan Mountain — the westernmost limit of human habitation — to welcome the dead on their arrival in the other world. Those who understood how to beseech her aid by means of the prescribed formulas she would carry in safety on her back to the after world.

She was also called 'the Lady of the Sycamore', for she would sometimes hide in the foliage of this tree on the edge of the desert and appear to the dead with the bread and water of welcome. It

Right: The god Amon in the form of a ram wearing a triple crown. Above him rises the goddess Uatchit as a winged uraeus.

Rameses IX and the goddess Hathor with the emblem of the sistrum on her head. From Thebes.

The hypostyle, Karnak.

Right: *Papyrus of Ani. It shows Hathor in the centre as a hippopotamus, and on the right as a cow standing guard over Ani's tomb. British Museum.*

was she, they believed, who held the long ladder by which the deserving could climb to heaven. More and more the goddess specialised in her role of funerary deity until in the last epoch a dead person was no longer called 'an Osiris' but 'a Hathor'.

Her principal sanctuary was at Dendera where she was worshipped in company with her husband, Horus of Edfu, who here ceded first place to her, and with their son Ihy (Ahy), 'the Sistrum Player', who is represented as an infant jingling the sistrum at her side. When Hathor was considered as a mother-goddess, in which role she was sometimes confused with Nut and Isis, Ihy became the 'bull of confusion', the symbol of light and fresh beginnings — thus being identified with the sun. Great festivals were celebrated in the temple of Dendera, above all on New Year's Day, which was the anniversary of her birth. Before dawn the priestesses would bring Hathor's image out on to the terrace to expose it to the rays of the rising sun. The rejoicing which followed was a pretext for a veritable carnival, and the day ended in song and intoxication. This was in memory of the occasion when Hathor, taking the form of Ra's Eye, nearly destroyed mankind; Ra succeeded in stopping her only by spreading blood-coloured beer on the fields. Hathor, pausing to admire her reflection in the beer, drank it and became too drunk to pursue her intention of massacring mankind.

Where Hathor was worshipped in Somaliland, she was called 'Mistress of the land of Punt', and perhaps had come from there in very ancient times. In the Sinai peninsula she was known as 'Mistress of the land of Mefket'; and in Phoenicia, where part of the Osirian legend had early taken root, as 'the Lady of Byblos'.

Above: *Bas-relief showing the goddess Hathor and Seti I, a warrior king of the Nineteenth Dynasty. Louvre.*

Anubis

Anubis, the Greek rendering of Anpu, was identified with Hermes, Conductor of Souls. It was Anubis who opened for the dead the roads of the other world. He is represented as a black jackal with a bushy tail, or as a blackish-skinned man with the head of a jackal or the head of a dog, an animal sacred to Anubis. For this reason the Greeks called the chief city of his cult Cynopolis.

From the earliest dynasties Anubis presided over embalmments. Funeral prayers, in which he was always to occupy a preponderant position, were in those days almost exclusively addressed to him.

In the *Pyramid Texts* Anubis is the 'fourth son of Ra' and his daughter is Kebehut, the goddess of freshness. But later he was admitted into the family of Osiris and it was said that Nephthys, left childless by her husband Set, bore him adulterously to Osiris.

Abandoned by his mother at birth, he was, it is related, found by his aunt, Isis. Isis, feeling no rancour at the thoughtless infidelity of her husband, undertook to bring up the baby. When he had grown to man's estate Anubis accompanied Osiris on his conquest of the world, and when 'the Good One' was murdered he helped Isis and Nephthys to bury him.

It was on this occasion that Anubis invented funeral rites and bound up the mummy of Osiris to preserve him from contact with the air and subsequent corruption. He was known, therefore, as 'Lord of the Mummy Wrappings'. From then on he presided over funerals and it is in this role that we often see him, first proceeding with the mummy's embalming and later receiving it at the door of the tomb. Anubis also makes sure that offerings brought by the deceased's heirs actually reach him.

Afterwards we see Anubis take the dead by the hand and, acting in his capacity of usher to Osiris, introduce him into the presence of the sovereign judges before whom he then weighs the soul of the dead.

This role of god of the dead won Anubis a universal cult and his admission into the circle of Osiris kept his worship alive until the last epoch when, because of his identification with Hermes, Conductor of Souls, he was given the name Hermanubis. In the great procession in honour of Isis, which Apuleius describes, it is the dog-headed god, bearing in his hands the caduceus and the palms, who marches at the head of the divine images.

Above: *The mummy at the sepulchre, held by Anubis. From* The Book of the Dead. *British Museum.*

Right: *Funeral stela from the tomb of Ramose. Elaborate funeral rites were practised in which the family of the deceased played an important part. Here the brother of the dead man pours a libation. c. 1300 B.C.*

Left: *Anubis, usually represented with the head of a jackal, was the god who, with Upuaut, presided over the embalming of the dead and supervised the weighing of the heart against truth (represented by the goddess Mayet or her emblem, an ostrich feather).*

81

Upuaut

Upuaut (or Ophois Wepwawet) is a wolf-headed or jackal-headed god who must not be confused with Anubis. Upuaut signifies 'he who opens the way'. In prehistoric representations we see the wolf-god, borne high upon his standard, guiding the warriors of his tribe into enemy territory. Similarly during his principal procession, Upuaut, carried on his shield, leads the cortège at the festivals of Osiris. Sometimes he is also shown piloting the sun's boat during its nocturnal voyage and, if necessary, towing it along the edge of the southern and northern sky.

A former warrior-god, he was also worshipped as god of the dead; and notably at Abydos, before Osiris deposed him, he was worshipped as Lord of the Necropolis under the name Khenti Amentiu, 'he who rules the West'.

Upuaut was feudal god of Siut, the Greek Lycopolis, and a later addition to the Osirian legend. He was an ally of Osiris and, with Anubis, one of his chief officers during the conquest of the world. As such, they both sometimes appear in later times dressed as soldiers.

Thoth

Thoth is the form which the name Djehuti or Zehuti had taken in Graeco-Roman times. He was identified by the Greeks with Hermes, Messenger of the Gods, and was worshipped throughout Egypt as a moon-god, patron of science and literature, wisdom and inventions, the spokesman of the gods and their keeper of the records.

Djehuti seems merely to mean 'he of Djehut' the name of the old province in Lower Egypt whose capital, Hermopolis Parva, must have been the cradle of Thoth's cult before he had established his principal sanctuary at Hermopolis Magna in Upper Egypt.

Thoth is ordinarily represented with the head of an ibis, often surmounted by a crescent moon, or simply as an ibis. He liked to appear as a bird of this sort, but also at times as a dog-headed ape, which makes us suspect that the god of historical ages may have been derived from a fusion, in very remote times, of two lunar divinities, one conceived as a bird, the other as an ape, or baboon.

According to the theologians of Hermopolis, Thoth was the true universal Demiurge, the divine ibis who had hatched the world-egg at Hermopolis Magna. They taught that he had accomplished the work of creation by the sound of his voice alone. When he first awoke in the primordial Nun he opened his lips, and from the sound that issued forth four gods materialised and then four goddesses. For this reason the future Hermopolis was called Khnum, 'City of the Eight'. Without real personality these eight gods perpetuated the creation of the world by the word; and the texts tell us that they sang hymns morning and evening to assure the continuity of the sun's course.

In the *Pyramid Texts*, Thoth is sometimes the oldest son of Ra, sometimes the child of Geb and Nut, the brother of Isis, Set and Nephthys. Normally, however, he does not belong to the Osirian family and is only the vizier of Osiris and his kingdom's sacred scribe.

He remained faithful to his murdered master and contributed powerfully to his resurrection, thanks to the trueness of his voice which increased the force of his magic incantations, and to the thoroughness of the way in which he purified the dismembered body of Osiris. Afterwards he helped Isis to defend the child Horus against the perils which beset him. We are told how on the orders of the gods he drove out the poison from the child's body when he had been stung by a scorpion. Later we see him intervene in the merciless struggle between Horus and Set, curing the former's tumour and the latter's castration by spitting on their wounds. Finally, when the two irreconcilable enemies were summoned to appear before the tribunal of the gods sitting in Hermopolis, Thoth earned the title 'He who judges the two companions', for his was the voice of reason.

As he had been the vizier of Osiris, so afterwards was he that of Horus. When Horus resigned earthly power Thoth succeeded him to the throne. During three thousand two hundred and twenty-six years Thoth remained the very model of a peaceful ruler.

Endowed with complete knowledge and wisdom, Thoth invented all the arts and sciences: arithmetic, surveying, geometry, astronomy, soothsaying, magic, medicine, surgery, music with wind instruments and strings, drawing and, above all, writing, without which humanity would have run the risk of forgetting his doctrines and of losing the benefit of his discoveries.

As inventor of hieroglyphs, he was named 'Lord of Holy Words'. As first of the magicians he was

Left: *Statue of a baboon, the animal sacred to Thoth which is found embalmed at Thebes and Hermopolis.*

Below: *Thoth was both scribe of the lower regions and one of the earliest lunar deities. Usually a human figure with ibis head, he is also represented as a dog-headed ape, with a crescent moon or lunar disk on his head. British Museum.*

often called 'The Elder'. His disciples boasted that they had access to the crypt where he had locked up his books of magic, and they undertook to decipher and learn 'these formulas which commanded all the forces of nature and subdued the very gods themselves'. It is to this infinite power which his followers attributed to him that he owes the name Thoth — three times very, very great — which the Greeks translated as Hermes Trismegistus.

After his long reign on earth Thoth ascended to the skies where he had various functions.

First of all he was the moon-god, or at least the god in charge of guarding the moon; for this astral body had its own individuality and name: Aah-te-Huti. We have already recounted the legend (*see* Nut) which tells how Thoth played draughts with the moon and won a seventy-second part of its light from which he created the five intercalary days. Elsewhere we are told that the moon is the left eye of Horus, watched over by either an ibis or a dog-headed ape. On the other hand a passage in *The Book of the Dead* tells us that Ra ordered Thoth to take his own place in the sky while he himself 'lighted the blessed in the Underworld'.

The moon then appeared and in its boat began its nocturnal voyages, each month exposed to the attack of monsters who slowly devoured it but who, happily, were constrained by the moon's faithful champions to disgorge it.

In his function as lunar divinity Thoth measured time, which he divided into months (to the first of which he gave his own name) and into years, which in turn were divided into three seasons.

He was the divine regulative force and charged with all calculations and annotations. At Edfu we see him before the temple trinity presenting the register in which is recorded all that concerns the geographical division of the country, its dimensions and resources. At Deir el Bahri we see him proceeding scrupulously with an inventory of treasures brought to the gods of Egypt by a naval expedition on its return from the land of Punt.

Thoth was the keeper of the divine archives and at the same time the patron of history. He carefully noted the succession of the sovereigns and, on the leaves of the sacred tree at Heliopolis, wrote the name of the future pharaoh whom the queen had just conceived after union with the Lord of the Heavens. On a long palm shoot he also inscribed the happy years of reign which Ra had accorded to the king.

He was the herald of the gods and also often served as their clerk and scribe. 'Ra has spoken, Thoth has written', we read. And during the awful judgment of the dead before Osiris we see Thoth, who has weighed the heart and found it not wanting, proclaim in a loud voice the verdict 'not guilty' which he has just registered on his tablets.

He was invested with the confidence of the gods and chosen by them as arbiter. We have already seen him awarding judgment to Horus and condemning Set. Also, at least from the time of the New Empire, he everywhere replaces Set in coronation scenes, in scenes in which libations are offered to the king, and in the symbolic ceremony of *sam-taui*.

The texts often couple him with Mayet, the goddess of Truth and Justice; but in no temple do we find them together. On the other hand two spouses of his were known, Seshat and Nehmauit,

The obelisk to Queen Hatshepsut at Karnak.

'she who uproots evil'. In Heliopolis they form with him two triads with, in the first instance, Hornub as divine son, and in the second Nefer Hor.

Plutarch tells us that the chief festival of the ibis-headed god was celebrated on the nineteenth of the month of Thoth, a few days after the full moon at the beginning of the year. His friends were then approached with the words, 'Sweet is the Truth', and were presented with gifts.

Seshat

Seshat (or Sesheta) was Thoth's principal spouse. In reality she is, as goddess of writing and history, merely his double. At first she was portrayed with the features of a woman wearing on her head a star inscribed in a reversed crescent, surmounted by two long straight plumes, the hieroglyph of her name, which signifies 'the secretary'. Later, owing probably to a misunderstanding on the part of sculptors, the crescent was replaced by two long, turned-down horns, from which the goddess derived the title Safekh-Aubi, i.e. 'she who wears (or, perhaps, raises) the two horns'.

She was a stellar divinity who served to measure time; to her — as to Thoth — was ascribed the invention of letters. She was called 'Mistress of the house of books'.

She was also called 'Mistress of the house of architects' and was represented as the foundress of temples, helping the king to determine the axis of a new sanctuary by the aid of the stars, and marking out the four corners of the edifice with stakes.

As goddess of history and record-keeper for the gods, we see her, alone or in the company of her husband, writing the names of the sovereigns on the leaves of the sacred tree at Heliopolis, or registering on a long palm-leaf the years of reign accorded to the pharaoh and, on this occasion, drafting the minutes of jubilee celebrations.

As mistress of the scribes she writes on a tablet the balance due to the king from captured enemy booty. When the great sovereign of the Eighteenth Dynasty, Queen Hatshepsut, sends an expedition to the land of Punt it is Seshat who, on its return to Thebes, makes the inventory of the treasures brought back. 'Thoth made a note of the quantity', we are told, 'and Seshat verified the figures.'

Protective divinities of the pharaohs and the kingdom

In the course of this study we have already met several gods who enjoyed the especial favour of the kings who considered them to be their divine ancestors. Such were Set, formerly Lord of Upper Egypt, but later expelled from the Egyptian pantheon; Horus, of whom every pharaoh boasted that he was the living incarnation; and Ra, whose son each pharaoh from the Fifth Dynasty onwards proclaimed himself to be. We shall now review other gods in the chronological order in which their dynastic importance appears most marked.

Sekhmet, generally lion-headed, is the goddess of fire and symbolises the devouring fury of the sun, a force to be considered in a desert land. With Ptah and Imhotep she was a member of the Triad of Memphis. Karnak.

86

Nekhebet

Nekhebet, who was identified by the Greeks as
Illithyia, protectress of childbirth, was from the
earliest time the protective goddess of Upper
Egypt. The centre of her cult was at El Kab, the
former Nekheb, which the Greeks called Illithyias-
polis, capital of the oldest kingdom in the South.

In war and offertory scenes she often appears
hovering over the pharaoh's head in the form of
a vulture, holding in her claws the fly-whisk and
the seal.

She is also sometimes portrayed as a divinity
with the bald head of a vulture, or as a woman
wearing the white crown of Upper Egypt either
on her head or on a head-dress shaped like a
vulture.

As a mother-goddess Nekhebet suckled the
royal children; often we see her suckling the
pharaoh himself.

Buto

Buto, a transcription of Per Uadjit, 'the dwelling
of Uadjit', was the name which the Greeks gave
to the Delta town and also to the goddess who was
worshipped there. She was the ancient protectress
of Lower Egypt.

The Osirian legend recounts that Buto, sovereign of the Delta, allied herself with Isis and
helped protect her infant child. She gathered up
the baby Horus from the floating island of Chemmis, for which reason she was afterwards identified with Latona, the mother of Apollo.

Buto was a snake-goddess, frequently represented in the form of a cobra, sometimes winged
and sometimes crowned. She also often has the
features of a woman wearing, either directly on
her head or on a head-dress in the form of a vulture,
the red crown of the North, of which she was the
official protectress as Nekhebet was of the white
crown of the South.

The vulture-goddess and the cobra-goddess,
known conjointly as Nebti — 'the two mistresses'
— appear side by side on royal documents. Sometimes they embellish the pharaoh's forehead in
order to protect him against his enemies, though
normally only the *uraeus* appears.

Mont

Mont (Menthu) was the Theban god of war whom the Greeks, because of his solar character, identified with Apollo. He appears at the beginning of the Middle Kingdom when he was particularly venerated by the kings of the Eleventh Dynasty, many of whom took the name Menthu-hetep, 'Mont is satisfied'.

He is usually represented as a figure whose falcon head is surmounted by the solar disk and two tall straight plumes. At a later period he also appears as a man with a bull's head embellished with the same attributes. The bull was actually the animal sacred to him. The bull in which he preferred to become incarnate was the celebrated Buchis which was piously tended at Hermonthis, the sun's residence in Upper Egypt. Hermonthis was the former capital of this region and Mont, the sun-god, was for many long centuries its lord and master before he was demoted to second rank by his former vassal, Amon of Thebes, who became king of the gods.

Having ousted Mont, Amon, whose wife was barren, wished to adopt him as divine son in the Theban triad; but the former sovereign of the entire region could not long be happy in such a subaltern position. Mont therefore chose to dwell apart at Hermonthis, of which he remained the uncontested master, and at Medamud, in the outskirts of Thebes, where numerous votaries came to worship him in company with his wife Rat-taui.

A solar god of warlike character, Mont was represented as the god of war under the New Kingdom. He brandished the *khepesh*, which was a kind of very curved scimitar, and cut off the heads of the pharaoh's enemies. We see him offering the pharaoh his invincible weapon and leading his vanquished enemies in chains. Temple bas-reliefs also often show Mont as sun-god of the South, with Atum, sun-god of the North, escorting the king into the sanctuary.

Above: *Mont, lord of the sky and one of the deified attributes of the sun.* Right: *A limestone figure inscribed with the name of a devotee of Mont.*

88

Amon

Amon (Amun, Ammon) is the name of the great Egyptian deity who was often given the title 'king of the gods'. For this reason the Greeks identified him with Zeus. He was almost unknown in the time of the Old Kingdom. His name — which seems to be derived from a root meaning 'hidden' — appears only four times in the Heliopolitan *Pyramid Texts*, for at that time he was a purely local divinity of Thebes. Thebes, which afterwards was to erect such gigantic temples in his honour, was at that time only a village in the fourth nome (or province) of Upper Egypt, the capital of which was Hermonthis, city of Mont, who was then Lord of all that region.

It was with the first king of the Twelfth Dynasty, whose name Amenemhat signifies 'Amon leads', that Thebes and its god began to take on an importance which was to become considerable under the great conquerors of the Eighteenth Dynasty called Thuthmosis and Amenhotep, who proudly proclaimed themselves to be 'sons of Amon'.

Amon by this time had dispossessed Mont and become the great divinity of the whole country of which Thebes — which was called Nut Amon, the 'city of Amon', or simply Nut, 'the city' — was henceforth the capital.

Amon normally appears with bronzed human features wearing as a head-dress a kind of crown which supports two straight tall parallel plumes. Sometimes he is seated majestically on a throne. Sometimes he stands with a whip raised above his head, in the ithyphallic pose of the god Min.

He is also at times represented with the head of a ram with curled horns, and at Karnak an animal of this sort was religiously tended, a living incarnation of the god. They also kept a goose which was Amon's other sacred animal.

The phallic Amon represented the forces of generation and reproduction. He was often called 'his mother's husband' and was supposed to initiate and maintain the continuity of creative life. He was the god of fertility, and we see the king, in his presence, sowing grain and cutting the first sheaf.

He was the patron of the most powerful pharaohs; he acknowledged them as his sons and gave them victory over their enemies. It was then

quite natural that the god of Thebes should become pre-eminently the national god. The faithful proclaimed him 'king of the gods' under the name Amon-Ra; for when the theologians had obligingly identified him with Ra, the old sun-god, Amon assumed Ra's position as universal Demiurge and chief of the great Ennead. Pictured in the royal tombs we see Amon-Ra enthroned in the sun's boat and, during the twelve hours of night, illuminating the Underworld.

Ra, however, had never abdicated his ancient authority, and under the name of Ra-Harahkte he always enjoyed his own distinct cult. Indeed, under the reign of Amenhotep III, there was a reaction in Ra's favour, no doubt encouraged by the priests of Heliopolis who were jealous of Amon's immense fortune and the omnipotence which this parvenu among the gods claimed. The texts and bas-reliefs on the walls of the temple of Luxor glorify the divine birth of Amenhotep as a result of Amon's love for the queen-mother, wife of Thuthmosis IV. But on the death of Amenhotep the cult of Ra-Harakhte gained new importance. Under the already venerable name 'Aten of the Day' — i.e. 'the solar disk whence issues the light of day', his visible form and true name — it

Part of the avenue of the sphinxes leading to the Great Temple of Amon at Karnak, near Thebes.

The god Amon, in the form of a ram, protects one of the faithful, who stands with his back to the breast of the god.

Below: *Part of a tablet bearing the title of Sesostris I in the temple of Amon at Karnak. The bee formed part of the hieroglyph of his name.*

seems that Ra-Harakhte engaged in a struggle against his rival Amon which was so successful that Amon was momentarily humbled. In the fourth year of his reign Amenhotep's son and successor proclaimed a great religious reform and decreed that only the religion of Aten or Aton was official.

Full of zeal for his new god, the reforming pharaoh began by changing his name Amenhotep ('Amon is satisfied') to Akhenaton ('The glory of Aton'). He hastened to abandon Thebes for a new capital city, Akhetaten — the present-day Tell-el-Amarna — which he had built in Middle Egypt to the glory of the solar disk.

There were no statues of Aten. Bas-reliefs and paintings always represent him in the form of a great red disk from which fan out long rays tipped with hands which have seized offerings laid on altars, or which present to the king, the queen

90

and their daughters the hieroglyphs of life and strength. The pharaoh was his only priest, and his cult was celebrated in a temple resembling ancient solar temples of the Old Kingdom and called, like the celebrated sanctuary of Ra at Heliopolis, Het Benben, 'the Palace of the Obelisk'. There, at the extremity of a vast courtyard, rose the obelisk of the sun. The ceremony consisted of an oblation of fruits and cakes and the recitation of hymns of great beauty, which were composed by the king himself in honour of his god. In them the sun was glorified, as in olden days, as creator of mankind and benefactor of the world, but without those allusions to early mythological legends of which the ancient hymns to Ra had been full. The hymns could thus be sung and understood not only by the inhabitants of the Nile valley but also by foreigners. All men, they proclaimed, were equally the children of Aten. In this modified attempt at monotheism we may suspect plans for an Empire-wide religion, especially if it is remembered that at this time Egyptian domination extended as far as Asia, where the Syrians worshipped Adonis and the Jews worshipped Adonai.

As long as the king lived there was no official god in Egypt but Aten. The other gods were proscribed and bitter war declared against them, especially against Amon and his trinity. Their temples were despoiled and their riches given to the solar disk. Their statues were broken and the bas-reliefs on which they appeared were mutilated, while Amon's name was harried from the most inaccessible places. It was chiselled off and removed from all the royal tablets, even from those of Amenhotep III, the pharaoh's own father.

The new religion, it is true, was ephemeral, and on the death of the reformer, or very shortly afterwards, his own son denied his father's name and restored the cult of Amon. He changed his heretical name Tut-ankh-Aten ('Living image of Aten') into the orthodox Tut-ankh-Amon ('Living image of Amon'). Wherever it was found, the old name was replaced by the new. But there were oversights, and on the magnificent throne of the young pharaoh, recently removed from his celebrated tomb, we can still read the two names almost side by side — a silent witness to the prince's heresy and to its abjuration.

Restored to all his former splendour by Horemheb and the kings of the Nineteenth Dynasty, who heaped his temples with gifts, Amon, from

Amon-Ra, the great god of Thebes, in the form of Amenophis III, wearing the solar disk with two tall plumes. Unknown in the Old Kingdom, he later superseded Ra, the old sun-god, as king of the gods, patron of the pharaohs, and god of fertility. Eighteenth Dynasty.

now on incorporated with Ra, saw his fortune grow to such a point that it reached three-quarters of that of all the other gods combined. An inventory of his wealth made under Rameses III tells us that he possessed, among other riches, 81,322 slaves and 421,362 head of cattle. His high priests, the first prophets of Amon, were chosen from among the most powerful lords. They soon became hereditary and, after playing the role of royal comptrollers to the weak sovereigns of the Twentieth Dynasty, finally seized the crown itself. Herihor, the priest, succeeded the last Rameses to the throne. During the troubles that ensued Thebes ceased to be the royal seat and political capital of Egypt. It remained from then on the exclusive property of Amon and became a kind of theocratic state where the god wielded power, either directly through his oracles or by the mediation, no longer as in the past of his chief prophet, but of his earthly spouse. This was normally the king's daughter, 'the god's wife', 'the god's adorer'. She was paid the highest honour, ruled the town and administered the immense domains of the god, her husband.

Sovereign of Thebes, Amon extended his power beyond the frontiers of Egypt into Ethiopia where, through his oracles at Napata and Meroe, he himself chose the kings. He deposed them and ordered their death, thus exercising a tyrannical domination which ended only in the third century B.C. when Ergamenes threw off the priests' yoke and had them put to death.

Amon's power over the desert tribes of Libya was equally great and until the latest period pilgrims crowded in great numbers to that venerable oasis-temple of Amon — or of Jupiter Ammon — where the celebrated oracle had, in 332 B.C., saluted Alexander the Great and called him 'Son of Amon'. This incident was a turning point in the career of Alexander and was to be of great future consequence in the formulation of the theory of divine kingship outside Egypt.

Amon's most magnificent sanctuaries were, however, at Thebes on the right bank of the Nile, at Luxor and at Karnak, whose ruins today still fill us with admiration, and where he was worshipped in company with Mut, his wife, and their son Khons. On the bas-reliefs which cover the walls and columns we see the king of the gods on his throne, where he receives the perpetual adoration of the pharaoh, whom at times he embraces and whom he infuses with the vital fluid *ka*. Elsewhere he gives the breath of life to him and grants him long years of reign. He hands him the *khepesh* of battle and, trampling the vanquished underfoot, delivers over enemy towns. Finally Amon is shown holding on his knees the queen on whom he will father the next pharaoh, his son.

Left: *Amenhotep IV (the heretical Akhenaton) and his wife worshipping the sun-god Aten or Aten-Ra, whose rays bear hands with which to receive offerings. Eighteenth Dynasty.*

Ra, the sun-god, in the solar barque with the sun. Together they traverse the heavens on their daily course. Papyrus of Ani from the Theban Book of the Dead. *British Museum.*

Mut

Mut, being Amon-Ra's wife, was identified by the Greeks with Hera. She is a vague and ill-defined deity whose name signified 'Mother'. She is represented as a woman wearing a head-dress in the form of a vulture, the hieroglyph of her name. Again she wears a heavy wig surmounted by the *pschent* — the double crown to which as wife of the king of the gods she had a right.

She grew in stature along with her spouse and when he, under the name Amon-Ra, had become the great god of the heavens she also became a solar deity. She was sometimes identified with Bast, whose cat-form she assumed; and with Sekhmet, from whom she borrowed the head of a lioness.

A text tells us that as a sky-goddess she remained — in the form of a cow — behind Amon when he emerged from the waves and broke from the egg at Hermopolis. 'He mounted on her back, seized her horns, and dismounted where it pleased him so to do.'

When she had long been childless Mut first adopted Mont, then Khons. It is with Khons as child that she entered the celebrated Theban triad of which Amon was the chief.

The head of Queen Akmet, mother of Hatshepsut. A relief from the tomb of Queen Hatshepsut at Deir el Bahri.

Left: *Mut and Amon, two members of the Great Triad of Thebes (the third was Khons). Mut, the mother of the gods, is often represented with the emblem of a vulture, this being a symbol associated with maternity.*

Right: *Sesostris I embraced by Ptah. Detail from a pillar.*

*Nile deity with offering trays. Relief on sandstone
pillar. Temple of Rameses at Abydos.*

The protective goddess Selket at one corner of the   97
gilded wooden shrine of Tut-ankh-Amon.

Khons

Khons (Khensu), whose name means 'the Navigator' or 'He who crosses the sky in a boat', seems originally to have been a moon-god, little known beyond the region of Thebes. It is a puzzle why the Greeks sometimes identified him with Hercules.

Khons is ordinarily represented in the form of a figure swathed like Ptah, whose composite sceptre he holds before him. His head is completely shaven except for one temple which is adorned by the heavy tress of a royal child. He wears a skullcap surmounted by a disk in a crescent moon. At first rather obscure, Khons rose to the ranks of the great gods when he was adopted by Amon and Mut and replaced Mont as their son in the Theban triad. It is only under the New Kingdom, however, that he seems to have begun to enjoy great popularity as an exorcist and healer. The possessed and the sick from all over Egypt and even from abroad had recourse to him. In the case of those from abroad Khons delegated his powers to a statue in which he incarnated a double of himself, commanding it to go forth and cure his suppliants. Thus we see the great Khons Neferhotep of Karnak, whose aid the Syrian prince of Bakhtan had implored on behalf of his daughter, delegate a second Khons in Syria who was named 'He who executes the designs and who expels the rebels'. Space is lacking to recount in detail how the divine substitute accomplished his mission and drove from the princess's body the demon which had tormented her; how at the end of three years and nine months he appeared in a dream to her father in the form of a golden falcon who flew swiftly towards Egypt; and how the grateful prince then hastened to take back the divine statue with the greatest ceremony together with costly gifts which were deposited in the temple of Karnak at the feet of the great Khons Neferhotep.

Khons was much venerated at Thebes and also worshipped at Ombos, where he formed the third person in the triad of Sebek under the name Khons Hor, who was represented as a man with a falcon's head surmounted with a disk in a crescent moon.

Left: *Coloured relief of the young Rameses II dedicating a statue. Temple of Rameses at Abydos.*

Right: *Head of Khons, one of the Theban Triad, with a sceptre. Granite. Late Eighteenth Dynasty.*

Khons is usually represented as a swathed figure. But at Ombos, as Khons Hor, he is given a falcon's head and shown with disk and crescent moon, which gives him some resemblance to the moon-god, Thoth.

Sebek

Sebek (in Greek, Suchos) is the name of a crocodile divinity who figured among the patrons of the kings of the Thirteenth Dynasty, many of whom were called Sebekhotep, 'Sebek is satisfied'.

The god was represented either as a man with the head of a crocodile or simply as a crocodile. In a lake attached to his chief sanctuary an actual crocodile was kept. It was called Petesuchos, 'He who belongs to Suchos' (or to Sebek), and it was said that the god was incarnate therein.

We know little of the origins of Sebek. A pyramid text calls him the son of Neith. But it is easy to conceive that the presence near by of a swamp or a rock-encumbered rapid could have suggested to the inhabitants of the Fayyum of Ombos that the crocodile was the supreme god who must be appeased by sacrifice and prayers. To his worshippers no doubt Sebek was none other than the Demiurge who, on the day of creation, issued from the dark waters where until then he had reposed, in order to arrange the world — as the crocodile emerges from the river to deposit her eggs on the bank. Possibly because the name Sebek sounds in Egyptian a little like Geb he was sometimes given Geb's titles.

Sebek was especially venerated in the Fayyum. The whole province was under his protection and his principal sanctuary was in the former Shedet, the Crocodilopolis of the Greeks. We shall have occasion to speak further of this when we study the animals sacred to the Egyptians.

Sebek was the object of a cult in Upper Egypt also. One can still see today at Kom Ombo — the former Ombos — ruins of the temple where Sebek's triad was worshipped, as was a second triad of which Horus was the chief. Perhaps here Sebek really replaced the former Lord, Set the Ombite, whom the pious worshippers of Horus would not tolerate. What is certain is that Sebek often shared Set's evil reputation. He was reproached with having aided the murderer of Osiris when Set, to escape punishment for his crime, took refuge in the body of a crocodile. That was why these animals, worshipped in certain provinces, were mercilessly hunted down and destroyed in others.

Ptah

Ptah of Memphis, in his aspect of protector of artisans and artists, was identified by the Greeks with Hephaestus. He is normally represented as a mummified figure, often raised on a pedestal inside the *naos* of a temple, his skull enclosed in a tight head-band and his body swathed in mummy-wrappings. Only his hands are free and hold a composite sceptre uniting the emblems of life, of stability and of omnipotence.

He was worshipped from the earliest times at Memphis where, south of the ancient 'White Wall' of Menes, he possessed the celebrated temple of Ptah south of the Walls. Ptah must always have been of first importance as sovereign god of the old capital of the North, the city where the pharaohs were crowned. But little is known of his role before the advent of the Nineteenth Dynasty, whose great kings Seti I and Rameses II held him in particular devotion, while one sovereign of the same dynasty bore the name Siptah, which signified 'Son of Ptah'.

It was, however, after the extinction of the last of the Rameses, when the political role of the Delta had become predominant, that the god of Memphis attained his full glory. Of all the gods of Egypt he was then third in importance and wealth, yielding only to Amon and Ra; and not even to them in the estimation of his own priests, who proudly proclaimed him to be the Universal Demiurge who had with his own hands fashioned the world, the other gods being mere personifications of aspects of Ptah.

Ptah was the patron of artisans and artists and the inventor of the arts. He was at the same time designer, smelter of metal and builder. His high priest at Memphis bore a title analogous to the 'Master Builder' of our medieval cathedrals. It was he who during the construction of a temple directed architects and masons.

Today there remain only shapeless ruins of the celebrated temple of Memphis where priests showed Herodotus the ex-votos commemorating the great miracles performed by Ptah. Among others was the occasion on which he had saved Pelusium from Sennacherib's attacking Assyrians by raising an army of rats, who forced the assailants to retreat by gnawing their bowstrings, quivers, and the leather thongs of their shields.

In this temple Ptah was worshipped in company with his consort Sekhmet and their son Nefertum, who was later succeeded by Imhotep, a human hero deified. Near the sanctuary was piously tended the celebrated bull Apis, a living incarnation of the god.

Although Ptah was apt to be called 'fair of face' he is sometimes depicted as a deformed dwarf with twisted legs, hands on hips and a huge head, shaved except for the lock of childhood. Thus represented Ptah plays the role of protector against noxious animals and against all kinds of evils. He was early identified with the very ancient and obscure earth-god Tenen, the primeval mound, and also with Seker, of whom we shall speak briefly below. He was frequently invoked under the names Ptah Tenen or Tatenen, Ptah Seker and even Ptah Seker Osiris.

Seker

Seker (the Greek rendering is Sucharis) was doubtless a vegetation god before he became the god of the dead in the Memphis necropolis. There, in the form of a greenish hawk-headed mummy, he was worshipped in a sanctuary called Ro Stau, 'the doors of the corridors', which communicated directly with the Underworld. He was early identified with Osiris and brought to Osiris all his own local worshippers. It was under the name Seker Osiris that the god of the dead was usually worshipped in Memphis. In the end the great funerary divinity became Ptah Seker Osiris.

Ptah, according to Memphite teaching architect of the Universe and god of creation, who achieved pre-eminence with the political success of the Delta. He is generally depicted as a mummified figure, holding in his hand the staff of purity and the emblems of life and stability.

Sekhmet

Sekhmet (rendered in Greek as Sakhmis) is the name of the terrible goddess of war and battle who is usually represented as a lioness or a woman with the head of a lioness.

Her name, which means 'the Powerful', is simply a title of Hathor which was given to Hathor on the occasion when in the form of a lioness she hurled herself on the men who had rebelled against Ra. As we have already seen she attacked them with such fury that the sun-god, fearing the extermination of the human race, begged her to arrest the carnage. 'By thy life', she answered him, 'when I slay men my heart rejoices', and she refused to spare her victims. For this reason she was later given the name Sekhmet and represented in the form of a savage lioness. In order to save what remained of the human race Ra had recourse to a stratagem. He spread across the bloody battlefield seven thousand jugs containing a magic potion composed of beer and pomegranate juice. Sekhmet, who was thirsty, mistook this red liquid for human blood and drank it so avidly that she became too drunk to continue the slaughter. The human race was saved; but to appease the goddess, Ra decreed that 'on that day there should be brewed in her honour as many jugs of the philtre as there were priestesses of the sun'. This was henceforth done annually on the feast day of Hathor. The great massacre had taken place on the twelfth day of the first month of winter; thus the calendar of lucky and unlucky days carefully notes: 'Hostile,

101

hostile, hostile is the 12th Tybi. Avoid seeing a mouse on this day; for it is the day when Ra gave the order to Sekhmet.'

The goddess was called 'the beloved of Ptah'; for, though originally a divinity of Letopolis, she joined the Memphis triad as Ptah's wife, bearing him a son, Nefertum.

Attached to her cult were bone-setter.

Nefertum

Nefertum, which the Greeks rendered as Iphtimis, is the name of the original divine son of the Memphis triad. The Greeks identified him with Prometheus, perhaps because his father was said to be Ptah Hephaestus, the discoverer of fire.

He is habitually represented as a man armed with the curved sabre called the *khepesh*. His head is surmounted by an open lotus flower from which springs a horned stalk, and he often appears standing on a crouching lion. Sometimes he has the head of this lion, which he doubtless owes to his mother, the lion-goddess Sekhmet.

His name, which signifies 'Atum the Younger', clearly indicates that he was at first an incarnation of Atum of Heliopolis, a rejuvenated Atum who at dawn sprang from the divine lotus, asylum of the sun during the night. A native of Lower Egypt, he was considered as the son of Ptah, and his mother became that god's spouse. He therefore occupied the third place in the oldest Memphis triad.

Bast

Bast (Bastet) was identified by the Greeks with Artemis, probably by confusion with the lioness-headed goddess Tefnut. She was local goddess of Bubastis, capital of the eighteenth nome or province of Lower Egypt. Bubastis is a transcription of Per Bast, i.e. 'House of Bast'. She became the great national divinity when, about 950 B.C., with Sheshonk and the Libyan pharaohs of the Twenty-second Dynasty, Bubastis became the capital of the kingdom.

Though in origin a lioness-goddess, personifying the fertilising warmth of the sun, her sacred animal later became the cat, and she is represented as a cat-headed woman holding in her right hand either a sistrum or an aegis, consisting of a semi-circular breastplate surmounted with the head of a lioness. In her left hand she carries a basket.

She was related to the sun-god, whom some called her father and others her brother-spouse; and she became — like Sekhmet, with whom she is frequently confused in spite of their very dissimilar characters — the wife of Ptah of Memphis and with him formed a triad in which Nefertum was the third person.

Although, as patron of the kings of Bubastis, Bast had already become one of the great divinities of Egypt, it was in the fourth century B.C. that she achieved her greatest popularity. She existed also in secondary forms as Pekhet, the cat or lion-headed goddess of Speos Artemidos, to the east of Beni Hasan.

Left: *Gift offerings to the goddess Sekhmet, holding a sistrum. Before her stands a priest. To the right and left are the falcon and serpent symbols of Upper and Lower Egypt. Bronze inlaid with gold, silver and copper. c. 600 B.C.*

Right: *Lion-headed Sekhmet, goddess of vengeance and punisher of the damned in the Underworld. She was a member of the Great Triad of Memphis.*

Like Hathor she was a goddess of pleasure and loved music and the dance. She would beat time with the sistrum, often decorated with the figure of a cat, which she grasped in her hand. In her benevolence she also protected men against contagious disease and evil spirits.

Great and joyful festivals were periodically celebrated in her temple at Bubastis. Herodotus tells us that it was one of the most elegant in Egypt and recounts how the devout came in hundreds of thousands from all over the country for the huge annual fair. The journey, by barges, took place to the sound of flutes and castanets. Buffoonery and jokes were bandied between the pilgrims and the women on the banks of the river who watched the barges as they passed, and everything was a pretext for pleasantry and masquerade. On the appointed day a splendid procession wound through the town and festivities followed during which, it seems, more wine was drunk than during all the rest of the year.

To please the cat-goddess her devotees consecrated statues of this animal in great numbers, and in the shadow of her sanctuaries it was a pious custom to bury the carefully mummified bodies of cats who during their lifetime had been venerated as animals sacred to Bast.

Right: *Cat-headed Bast, wife of Ptah. Originally a lioness-goddess symbolising the fertilising warmth of the sun, she is frequently confused with Sekhmet. When Bubastis ('House of Bast') became capital of the kingdom in the Twenty-second Dynasty, she became a national deity.*

Far right: *Part of the basalt coffin of Uah-ab-Ra, overseer of the scribes of crown lands, inscribed with extracts from* The Book of the Dead *telling of the happiness to be found in the kingdom of Osiris. Twenty-sixth Dynasty. c. 600* B.C.

Neith

Neith (Neit), whom the Greeks identified with their Pallas Athene, is the name of a Delta divinity. She was protectress of Sais, which became capital of Egypt towards the middle of the seventh century B.C. when Psammetichus I, founder of the Twenty-sixth Dynasty, mounted the throne, thus assuring the wealth and importance of his local goddess.

She was, in fact, an extremely ancient divinity; for her fetish — two crossed arrows on an animal skin — was carried on the standard of a prehistoric clan, and two queens of the First Dynasty derived their names from hers.

Her epithet Tehenut, 'the Libyan', suggests that she probably originated in the west. She always remained important in Sais after having been, in very early times, perhaps, considered to be the national divinity of Lower Egypt, whose red crown she habitually wears. The crown was called 'Net', which sounds like her own name.

In the beginning she was worshipped in the form of a fetish composed of two crossed arrows on a shield or the mottled skin of an animal. Later she was represented with the features of a woman wearing the crown of the North and holding in her hand a bow and arrows. Still later her attribute became a weaver's shuttle, the hieroglyph of her name, which she sometimes wears on her head as a distinguishing emblem.

Neith, indeed, appears in a double role: as a warrior-goddess and as a woman skilled in the domestic arts. This is why she was identified with Athene, who also played this double role.

When, with the advent of the Saite dynasty, her pre-eminence was established, she played a part in many cosmogonic myths. She was made a sky-goddess like Nut and Hathor, and she was proclaimed to be mother of the gods in general and of Ra in particular 'whom she bore before childbirth existed'.

She was great weaver who wove the world with her shuttle as a woman weaves cloth. Under the name Mehueret she was the Celestial Cow who gave birth to the sky when nothing existed.

She was introduced into the Osirian cult and confused with Isis; she became protectress of the dead and we sometimes see her offering them the bread and water on their arrival in the other world.

Just as Isis and Nephthys are frequently found together in pictures and texts, so Neith often appears with Selket, either as guardian of the mummy and viscera of the dead, or as protectress of marriage.

Today nothing remains of her celebrated temple at Sais where, Plutarch tells us, could be read the following inscription: 'I am all that has been, that is, and that will be. No mortal has yet been able to lift the veil which covers me'.

To this sanctuary was annexed a school of medicine, 'The House of Life', directed by the priests. Later, under the Persians, Darius' Egyptian doctor boasted that he had reorganised this medical school under royal protection.

Divinities of river and desert

Khnum

Khnum (Khnemu), which was rendered in Greek as Khnoumis, was a god of the region of the First Cataract. He is portrayed as a ram-headed man with long wavy horns, unlike the curved horns of the ram-headed Amon.

He was a god of fecundity and creation and was originally worshipped under the form of a ram or a he-goat. Like all gods of this sort he doubtless symbolised the Nile which comes from the heavens to fertilise the earth and make it fruitful. His chief sanctuary was near the First Cataract, not far from the spot where the earliest Egyptians placed the source of their great river, on that island of Elephantine of which Khnum was proclaimed sovereign lord.

From his temple, where he received offerings in company with his two wives, Sati and Anukis — who were, as far as we know, childless — Khnum watched over the sources of the Nile.

Khnum means 'the Moulder' and it was taught that he had formerly fashioned the cosmic egg on his potter's wheel. At Philae, moreover, he was called the 'Potter who shaped men and modelled the gods'. We see him moulding the limbs of Osiris; for it was he, they said, who 'shaped all flesh — the procreator who engendered gods and men'.

In this aspect he presided over the formation of children in their mothers' wombs. Temple bas-reliefs show him fashioning the body of the young pharaoh on his sculptor's turn-table. At Armant this young pharaoh is none other than the son of Julius Caesar and Cleopatra, here identified with the divine child Harsomtus.

The celebrity of Khnum soon crossed the nearby frontier and penetrated Nubia, whose god Dedun was also a ram, or a ram-headed god. This facilitated the identification of the two gods and attracted new and numerous worshippers to the island of Elephantine.

Left: *Hapi Atur, God of the Nile. Because the river brought fertility to the lands of the valley, Hapi is often depicted with a woman's breasts.*

Right: *The God of the Sea. Limestone relief from the funerary temple of King Sahure at Abusir. Old Kingdom.*

Harsaphes

Harsaphes, the Greek rendering of Hershef, 'He who is on his lake', was the name of another ram-headed god, identified by the Greeks with Hercules. His principal sanctuary was at Heracleopolis Magna in the Fayyum. Probably a Nile god, like all ram-headed gods, Harsaphes was from the earliest times the object of great veneration; for already under the First Dynasty we see King Ousaphais consecrating a *naos* to him.

Sati

Sati (Satet) was one of Khnum's two wives and as such a guardian goddess of the Cataracts. Her name signifies 'She who runs like an arrow'. She is the Archer who lets fly the river's current with the force and rapidity of an arrow. She is represented as a woman wearing the white crown of the South, flanked by two long horns. Like Neith she often holds arrows and a bow in her hands. She was worshipped in the extreme south of Egypt, where her favourite abode was on the island of Seheil. She gave her name to the first nome of Upper Egypt which was called Ta Setet, the 'Land of Sati'. Its capital was Abu, 'City of the Elephant', the Elephantine of the Greeks, where Sati took her place in the temple in company with Anuket.

Anuket

Anuket (Anquet), the Greek for which was Anukis, was Khnum's second wife. She is represented as a woman wearing a tall plumed crown. Her name seems to mean 'the Clasper' — she who clasps the river bank and presses the Nile between the rocks of Philae and Syene. She was worshipped at Elephantine with Khnum and Sati as a regional goddess of the Cataracts. She liked to reside on the island of Seheil, which was consecrated to her.

The pyramid of Sneferu at Dahshur is only slightly smaller than the Great Pyramid of Cheops. Sneferu was a warrior king of the Fourth Dynasty.

Min

Min, whom the Greeks identified with Pan, was a very ancient god whose totem, a thunderbolt apparently, appeared at the top of old prehistoric standards. Wearing a crown surmounted by two tall straight plumes which seem to have been borrowed from Amon or else adopted by Amon from Min, Min is always represented standing with a flail raised in his right hand behind his head and always with phallus erect.

This latter trait seems to indicate that Min was originally considered by his priests to be the creator of the world. He is often identified with Horus; and we may wonder if his name was not in earlier days simply a special name for the sun-god.

Be this as it may, Min was in the classical epoch chiefly worshipped as god of the roads and protector of travellers in the desert. The principal centre of his cult was Coptos, a point of departure for trading expeditions. Their leaders, before

Hapi

risking themselves in the deserts, never failed to invoke the great local god Min, god of the eastern desert and 'Lord of Foreign Lands'.

He was worshipped also as a god of fertility and vegetation and protector of crops. On temple walls we see scenes from the ceremonies which were celebrated in his honour as harvest-god during the king's enthronement. We see the pharaoh offering him the first sheaf which he has just cut and we see the homage which is rendered to the white bull, sacred to Min.

As well as in Coptos he was worshipped in Akhmin, the former Chemmis, known as Panopolis to the Greeks, who identified Min with Pan. There in his honour gymnastic games were celebrated, and it is perhaps for this reason that the Greek historian Herodotus praised the inhabitants of Panopolis for being the only Egyptians who liked Greek customs.

Hapi was the name of the deified Nile, and should be distinguished from Hapy, son of Horus, who was the tutelary divinity of the Canopic jar containing the lungs. He is given the figure of a man, vigorous but fat, with breasts developed like those of a woman, though less firm and hanging heavily on his chest. He is dressed like the boatmen and fishermen with a narrow belt which holds in his massive belly. On his head he wears a crown made of aquatic plants — of lotus if he is the Nile of Upper Egypt, of papyrus if he represents the river in Lower Egypt.

In fact, Hapi had two roles: as the southern Nile and as the northern Nile. There were two corresponding goddesses who personified the river banks and they are sometimes seen standing with outstretched arms, as though begging for water which will render them fertile.

The Egyptians thought of the Nile as flowing from Nun, the primordial ocean which waters the visible as well as the invisible world. It was also said that Hapi resided near the First Cataract, on the Isle of Bigeh, in a cavern where he poured water to heaven and earth from his urns. Towards the middle of June the Nile would rise and the devotees of Osiris affirmed that the inundation — on the height of which depended the year's prosperity — was caused by Isis weeping for her husband, treacherously slain by his wicked brother Set. The suitable height of the inundation was, in Graeco-Roman times, fixed at sixteen cubits — as the sixteen infants which decorate the famous statue of the Nile in the Vatican indicate. In order that the river should attain this height the Egyptians would make offerings to Hapi in June, imploring him with fervour and singing hymns.

Apart from this, Hapi scarcely played a part in religion as such, and he was not connected with any theological system.

In temples he occupied a secondary role, and appears as a servant offering his river products to the great gods. On the foundations of buildings we often find long processions of alternate gods and goddesses who resemble Hapi and are known as 'Niles'. They represent the sub-divisions of the two Egypts bringing the products of all the provinces, in tribute to the Lord of the sanctuary.

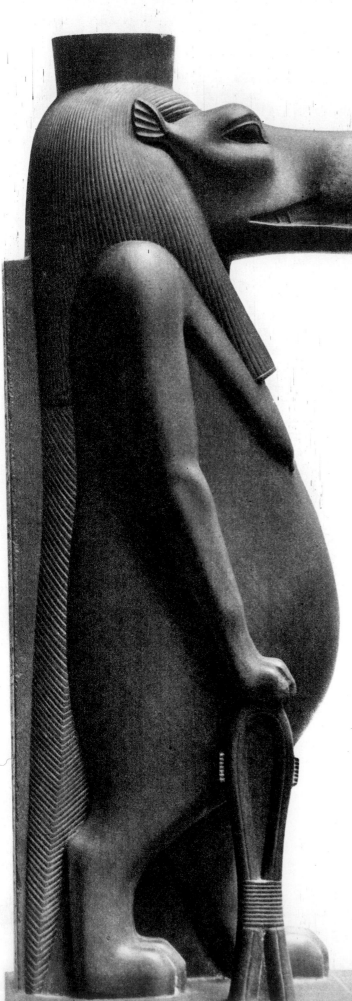

Minor divinities concerned with birth or death

Taueret

Taueret (Apet, Opet) 'the Great' was a popular goddess of childbirth and symbolised maternity and suckling.

She is represented as a pregnant hippopotamus with pendant mammae standing upright on her back legs and holding the hieroglyphic sign of protection, *ka*, a plait of rolled papyrus. Her head was partly that of a crocodile, her back was a crocodile's and she had lion's feet. She was especially worshipped in Thebes where, under the New Kingdom, she enjoyed great popularity among people of the middle class, who often gave her name to their children and decorated their houses with her images.

As well as her role of protectress Taueret sometimes fulfilled that of an avenging deity: then she would appear as a goddess with the body of a hippopotamus but the head of a lioness who brandished a dagger in a menacing manner.

Taueret, goddess of childbirth. Usually represented as a pregnant hippopotamus standing on her hind legs holding two plaits of rolled papyrus. Twenty-sixth Dynasty. Karnak.

Heket

Heket was a frog-goddess or a frog-headed goddess who, it seems, symbolised the embryonic state when the dead grain decomposed and began to germinate.

A primitive goddess, it was taught at Abydos that she came with Shu from the mouth of Ra himself and that she and Shu were the ancestors of the gods. She was, they also said, one of the midwives who assisted every morning at the birth of the sun. In this aspect she figures, like Nekhebet and others whom we shall mention, among the patrons of childbirth.

Meskhent

Meskhent is sometimes represented as a woman wearing on her head two long palm shoots, curved at their tips. She was a goddess of childbirth and personified the two bricks on which, at the moment of delivery, Egyptian mothers crouched. Sometimes we see Meskhent in the form of one of these bricks, terminated by a human head.

She appeared beside the expectant mother at the precise moment the baby was born; and she was said to go from house to house bringing relief to women in labour. Often, too, she played the role of fairy godmother and pronounced sentence on the newly born and predicted its future.

The old story in which the birth of the three first kings of the Fifth Dynasty is described permits us to determine the roles which these various divinities played during childbirth. When Reddedet approached the term of her confinement, Ra, the true father of the child she bore in her womb, ordered Isis, Nephthys, Heket and Meskhent to go to her bedside. The four goddesses, disguised as dancers and accompanied by Khnum who carried their luggage, set forth. When the moment had come Isis placed herself in front of Reddedet, Nephthys behind her, while Heket helped her. Isis received the child. The goddesses then washed it and placed it on a bed of bricks. Finally Meskhent approached the newborn baby and said: 'It is a king who will rule over all the land.' Khnum then put health and strength into its body.

Meskhent was one of the deities who appeared beside a dead man's soul when he came before Osiris for judgment, and she was expected to testify to his character.

Shai

Shai was 'Destiny', and was sometimes made a goddess Shait. He was born at the same moment as the individual, grew up with him and shadowed him until his death.

Shai's decrees were inescapable. When a man died and his soul came for judgment in the presence of Osiris, Shai could be seen in the form of a god without special attributes attending the trial in order to render exact account before the infernal jury of the deceased's virtues and crimes, or in order to prepare him for the conditions of a new life.

The Hathors

The Hathors were kinds of fairy godmothers who sometimes appeared at the birth of the young Egyptian to prophesy his inescapable destiny, much as we have seen Meskhent do. There were seven or even nine of them and we see them, in the form of young women, at the confinement of Ahmes at Deir el Bahri, of Mutemuia at Luxor and of Cleopatra at Armant.

Renenet

Renenet was the goddess who presided over the baby's suckling. She nourished him herself and also gave him his name — and, in consequence, his personality and fortune. At his death we see her with Shai when his soul is weighed and judged. She is variously represented: as a woman without attributes, as a snake-headed woman, as a woman with the head of a lioness, or as a *uraeus*, dressed and with two long plumes on her head. As a nursing goddess she symbolised nourishment. She gives her name to the month of Pharmuti, 'the month of Renenet', which was, in the later periods, the eighth month of the calendar.

Renpet

Renpet was the goddess of the year, the goddess of springtide and of youth. As a deity of time's duration she was called 'Mistress of Eternity'. She is represented as wearing above her head a long palm-shoot, curved at the end — the hieroglyph of her name.

Bes

Bes often appeared at birth, but chiefly he was a marriage-god and presided over the toilet of women.

Bes was a popular god who perhaps originated in the land of Punt of which he was sometimes called the Lord. He appears in the form of a robust dwarf of bestial aspect. His head is big, his eyes huge, his cheeks prominent. His chin is hairy and an enormous tongue hangs from his wide-open mouth. For head-dress he has a bunch of ostrich feathers; he wears a leopard skin whose tail falls behind him and is visible between his bandy legs. In bas-reliefs and paintings he is frequently represented full-face, contrary to the old Egyptian usage of drawing only in profile. He is normally immobile, hands on hips; occasionally, however, he skips cheerfully but clumsily and plays the harp or tambourine or, again, brandishes a broad dagger with a terrible and menacing air.

At once jovial and belligerent, fond of dancing and fighting, Bes was the buffoon of the gods. They delighted in his grotesque figure and contortions, just as the Memphite pharaohs of the Old Kingdom enjoyed the antics of their pygmies.

At first Bes was relegated to the lowest rank among the host of genii venerated by the common people, but his popularity grew; and under the New Kingdom the middle classes liked to place his statue in their houses and name their children after him.

From this epoch we often see Bes represented

Left: *Wooden figure of Ptai, who was charged with the care of the foetus. Fourteenth Dynasty. Louvre.*

Right: *Bes originates in Arabian mythology. He appears as a deformed dwarf with curly beard and leopard's tail and is variously the god of death, war and marriage. From his Herculean appearance, he is also called the god of strength. Sometimes he is seen playing with children. Louvre.*

in the *mammisi* of temples — that is to say, in the birth houses where divine accouchements took place. He thus presided over childbearing and at Deir el Bahri he appears with Taueret and other tutelary genii beside the queen's bed as a protector of expectant mothers.

He also presided over the toilet and adornment of women, who were fond of having his image carved on the handles of their mirrors, rouge boxes and scent bottles. Bed-heads are also frequently found ornamented with various representations of Bes; for he was the guardian of sleep who chased away evil spirits and sent the sleeper sweet dreams.

He was moreover an excellent protector not only against evil spirits but against dangerous beasts: lions, snakes, scorpions, crocodiles. Against their bite or sting the whole family could be preserved by taking care to place in the house a little stela or pillar, covered with magic formulas, on which was sculpted Bes' menacing mask above a figure of the infant Horus, standing on two crocodiles.

At the end of paganism Bes was even supposed to be the protector of the dead, and for this reason became as popular as Osiris.

After the triumph of Christianity Bes did not immediately vanish from the memory of man; for we are told of a wicked demon named Bes whom the holy Moses had to exorcise because he was terrorising the neighbourhood. To this day, it would seem, the monumental southern gate of Karnak serves as a dwelling-place for a knock-kneed dwarf whose gross head is embellished with a formidable beard. Woe to the stranger who, coming across him in the dusk of evening, laughs at his grotesque figure! For the monster will leap at his throat and strangle him. He is the Bes of ancient Egypt who, after long centuries, is not yet resigned to abandoning altogether the scenes of his earlier greatness.

Selket

Selket (Selquet) is the name of the old scorpion-goddess who was depicted as a woman wearing on her head a scorpion, the animal sacred to her. She was also at times a scorpion with a woman's head.

According to certain texts she was a daughter of Ra. She often played the role of guardian of conjugal union. At Deir el Bahri she appears with

Neith supporting the hieroglyph of the sky, above which Amon is united with the queen-mother. The two goddesses protect the couple from all disturbance.

Selket played an especial part in the ceremony of embalming, and with Isis, Nephthys and Neith guarded the Canopic jars containing the entrails of Osiris. She also helped Isis to look after the infant Horus.

As we have already noticed, Selket is often found in company with Neith, as Isis is with Nephthys. Like the other three goddesses Selket protected the dead, and like them we see her extending winged arms across the inner walls of sarcophagi.

Mertseger

Mertseger (Merseger), whose name signifies 'the Friend of Silence' or 'the Beloved of Him who makes Silence' (i.e. Osiris), was the name of a snake-goddess of the Theban necropolis. More accurately she pertained to one part of the funerary mountain at Thebes — the peak, shaped like a pyramid, which dominated the mountain chain and earned Mertseger the epithet Ta-dehnet, 'the peak'.

She is represented as a human-headed snake or even as a snake with three heads: namely, a human head surmounted by a disk flanked by two feathers between two others: a snake's head similarly embellished and a vulture's head. Although Mertseger was benevolent she could also punish. We have the confession of Neferabu, a modest employee at the necropolis, who admits to having been justly stricken with illness for his sins Afterwards he proclaims that he has been cured by 'the Peak of the West', having first repented and ardently besought her forgiveness.

Right: *Mayet, goddess of truth and justice.*

114

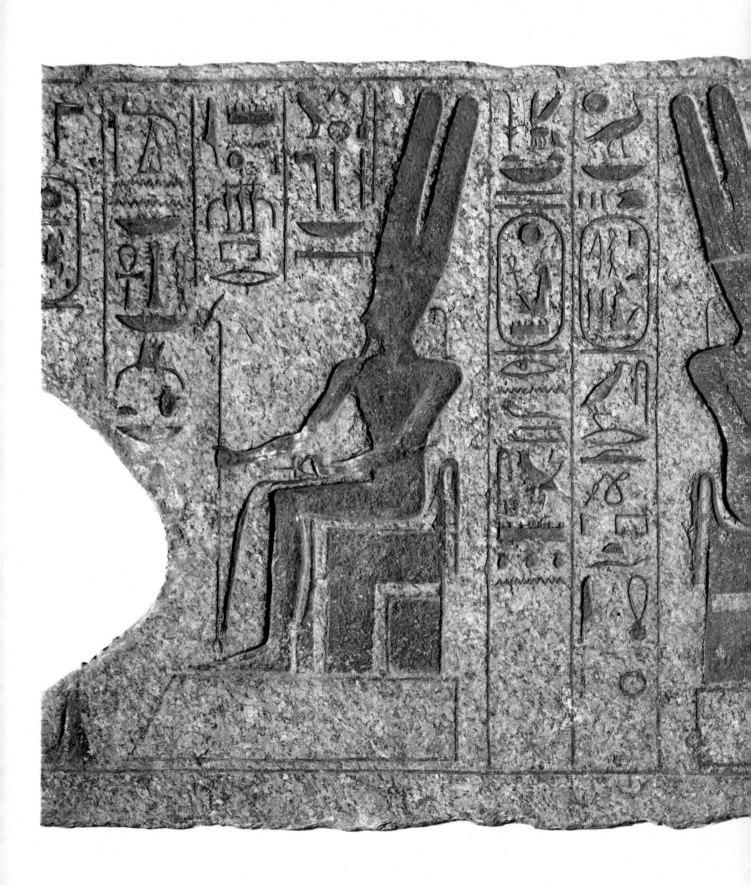

Left: *Painting from the Papyrus of Ani showing   Amon-Ra receiving offerings from Amenhotep II.   117
Ra and the Herd of Heaven.*

Girl attendants at Pennut's funeral. Part of a wall engraving from the Tomb of Pennut at Aniba.

Right: Porcelain figures of the four sons of Horus, divine guardians of the Canopic jars: jackal-headed Duamutef, falcon-headed Qebehsenuf, human-headed Imset and dog-headed Hapy.

The four sons of Horus

The four sons of Horus, who were members of the Third Ennead, were supposed to have been born to Isis; but it was also said that Sebek, on Ra's orders, caught them in a net and took them from the water in a lotus flower. It is on a lotus flower that they stand before the throne of Osiris during the judgment of the dead.

They were appointed by their father, Horus, to guard the four cardinal points. He also charged them to watch over the heart and entrails of Osiris and to preserve Osiris from hunger and thirst.

From then on they become the official protectors of viscera. Since the time of the Old Kingdom it had been usual to remove the viscera from the corpse, to separate them and preserve them in the so-called 'Canopic' jars.

Thus the human-headed Imset watched over the jar containing the liver; the dog-headed Hapy guarded the lungs; the jackal-headed Duamutef protected the stomach; and the hawk-headed Qebehsenuf had charge of the intestines.

Ament

Ament, whose name is a simple epithet meaning 'the Westerner', is represented as a goddess wearing an ostrich feather on her head or sometimes an ostrich plume and a hawk.

This feather, the normal ornament of Libyans, who wore it fixed in their hair, was also the sign for the word 'Western' and was naturally suitable to Ament, who was originally the goddess of the Libyan province to the west of Lower Egypt.

Later 'the West' came to mean the Land of the Dead, and the goddess of the West became the goddess of the dwelling-place of the dead.

At the gates of the Other World, at the entrance of the desert, one often sees the dead being welcomed by a goddess who half-emerges from the foliage of the tree she has chosen to live in to offer him bread and water. If he drinks and eats he becomes the 'friend of the gods' and follows after them, and can never return. The deity who thus welcomes the dead is often Ament, though she may frequently be Nut, Hathor, Neith or Mayet, who take their turn in replacing the goddess of the West.

119

Mayet

Mayet is depicted as a woman standing or sitting on her heels. On her head she wears the ostrich feather which is the hieroglyph of her name — truth or justice. She was the goddess of law, truth and justice. The texts describe her as the cherished daughter and confidante of Ra, and also the wife of Thoth, the judge of the gods who was also called 'the Master of Mayet'.

She formed part of the retinue of Osiris, and the chamber in which the god held his tribunal was named the 'Hall of Double Justice', for Mayet was often doubled into two absolutely identical goddesses who stood one in each extremity of the vast hall. Mayet also took her place in one pan of the balance opposite the heart of the dead in order to test its truthfulness.

In reality Mayet was a pure abstraction deified. The gods, it was taught, loved to nourish themselves on truth and justice. Thus, in the ritual of the cult, it was the offering of Mayet which genuinely pleased them; and in the temples we see the king, at the culminating point of divine office, presenting to the god of the sanctuary a tiny image of Mayet — an offering which was more agreeable to him than all the others he had received, no matter how rich they may have been.

Neheh

Neheh (Heh), 'Eternity', is another deified abstraction. The god of eternity is represented as a man squatting on the ground in the Egyptian manner and wearing on his head a reed, curved at the end. We often see him thus, carved on furniture and other homely objects, holding in his hands the sign for millions of years and various emblems of happiness and longevity.

Left: *The lady Maï.*

Right: *Painted limestone block statue of Amenhotep. Thebes. Eighteenth Dynasty.*

Imhotep

Imhotep, in Greek Imuthes, signifies 'He who comes in peace'. Imhotep was by far the most celebrated among those ancient sages who were admired by their contemporaries during their lifetime and after their death finally worshipped as equals of the gods.

Imhotep was vizier at the court of the ancient King Djoser of the Third Dynasty. He was Djoser's greatest architect and Djoser was the constructor of the oldest of the pyramids. During his reign the stone column seems to have been employed for the first time in the history of architecture.

By the time of the New Kingdom Imhotep was already famous. He was reputed to have written the *Book of Temple Foundations*, and under the pharaohs of Sais his popularity increased from year to year. Some time later,

The Step Pyramid at Sakkara. It rises in six steps and stands some 200 feet high.

Left: *Imhotep, the architect of the Step Pyramid, the oldest pyramid and the tomb of King Djoser at Sakkara. He was deified by later generations and venerated for his wisdom.*

during the Persian domination, it was claimed that Imhotep was born not of human parents but of Ptah himself. He was introduced into the triad of Memphis with the title 'Son of Ptah', thus displacing Nefertum.

He is represented with shaven head like a priest, without the divine beard, crown or sceptre and dressed simply as a man. He is generally seated or crouching, and seems to be attentively reading from a roll of papyrus laid across his knees.

He was patron of scribes and the protector of all who, like himself, were occupied with the sciences and occult arts. He became the patron of doctors. Then — for ordinary people who celebrated his miraculous cures — he became the god or, more accurately, the demi-god of medicine. He was thus identified by the Greeks with Asclepius. Towards the end of paganism Imhotep seems even to have relegated his father Ptah to second rank, and to have become the most venerated god in Memphis.

Amenhotep

Amenhotep, son of Hapu, whom the Greeks called Amenophis, was a vizier of Amenhotep III and lived in Thebes in the fifteenth century B.C.

'A sage and an initiate of the holy book', we are told, 'Amenhotep had contemplated the beauties of Thoth.' No man of his time better understood the mysterious science of the rites. He was remembered by the Thebans for the superb edifices he had had built. Among these, one of the most imposing was the funerary temple of the king, his master, of which today there remain only the two statues that embellished the façade. They are gigantic statues and one of them was renowned throughout antiquity under the name of the Colossus of Memnon. Throughout the centuries the renown of Amenhotep continued to grow. In the Saite period he was considered to be a man 'who, because of his wisdom, had partaken of the divine nature'. Magic books were attributed to him and miraculous stories told about him.

In the temple of Karnak there were statues of Amenhotep, son of Hapu, to which divine honours were paid; but he never became a true god like Imhotep, son of Ptah. He was, however, venerated in company with the great divinities in the little Ptolemaic temple of Deir el Medineh.

The old sage is generally portrayed as a scribe, crouching and holding on his knees a roll of papyrus.

Mask from the mummy of Tut-ankh-Amon. Of outstanding craftsmanship, it is made of beaten gold and inlaid with glass and precious stones. The head bears a cobra uraeus. Eighteenth Dynasty.

Pharaoh

Pharaoh must also be named among the gods of Egypt; for the king's divinity formed part of the earliest dogmas. To his subjects, moreover, he was the sun-god, reigning on earth. He wore the sun-god's *uraeus* which spat forth flame and annihilated his enemies. All the terms which were used in speaking of him, of his palace and of his acts could apply equally to the sun. It was taught that he actually perpetuated the solar line; for the god Ra took the form of the pharaoh to beget each successor to the throne.

In temples, and particularly those of Nubia, many ancient kings and the living king himself were often worshipped in company with the great gods. Thus we sometimes see pictures of the reigning pharaoh worshipping his own image.

Left: *Wood mask from the sarcophagus of Seti I, son of Rameses I and a pharaoh of the Nineteenth Dynasty (1312—1290 B.C.).*

Top right: *Cleopatra with the disk and horns of Hathor on her head. A relief in the temple of Hatshepsut at Deir el Bahri.*

Bottom right: *Giant statues of Rameses II seated on either side of the entrance to his tomb at Abu Simbel.*

The sacred animals

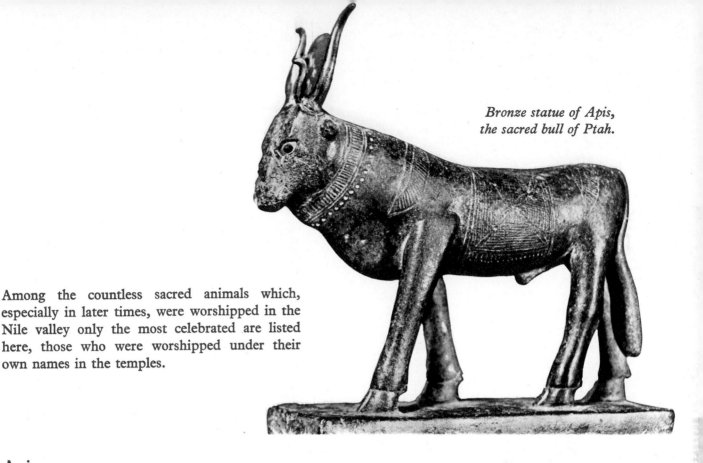

Among the countless sacred animals which, especially in later times, were worshipped in the Nile valley only the most celebrated are listed here, those who were worshipped under their own names in the temples.

Apis

Apis is a Greek rendering of Hapi. The bull Apis is today the best known of the sacred animals. Very popular and honoured throughout Egypt, he was tended and worshipped at Memphis, where he was called 'the Renewal of Ptah's life'. He was Ptah's sacred animal and believed to be his reincarnation. Ptah in the form of a celestial fire, it was taught, inseminated a virgin heifer and from her was himself born again in the form of a black bull which the priests could recognise by certain mystic marks. On his forehead there had to be a white triangle, on his back the figure of a vulture with outstretched wings, on his right flank a crescent moon, on his tongue the image of a scarab and, finally, the hairs of his tail must be double.

As long as he lived Apis daintily fed in the temple which the kings had had built for him in Memphis opposite the temple of Ptah. Every day at a fixed hour he was let loose in the courtyard attached to his temple, and the spectacle of his frolics attracted crowds of the devout. It also drew the merely curious; for a visit to the sacred animals was a great attraction for the tourists who were so numerous in Egypt during the Graeco-Roman era.

Each of his movements was interpreted as foretelling the future; and when Germanicus died it was remembered that the bull, shortly before this, had refused to eat the delicacies which Germanicus had offered him.

Normally, Apis was allowed to die of old age. Marcellinus Ammianus, however, tells us that if he lived beyond a certain age he was drowned in a fountain. During the Persian tyranny the sacred bull was twice assassinated, by Cambyses and by Ochus. Space is lacking to describe how the Egyptians mourned the death of Apis, and their transports of joy at the announcement that his successor had been found. Vast subterranean chambers have been discovered at Sakkara where the mummified bodies of the sacred bulls were, after splendid funeral services, buried in immense monolithic sarcophagi of sandstone or pink granite.

Above these galleries was a great temple of which today nothing remains, where the funeral cult of the dead bull was celebrated. He had become, like all the dead, an 'Osiris' and was worshipped under the name Usar-Hapi, or Osiris Apis. This in Greek was Osorapis, which caused him quickly to be confused with the foreign god Serapis. The hybrid god was worshipped according to a purely Greek ritual in the great Sarapeum at Alexandria. A god of the Underworld, Serapis was mingled at Memphis with Osorapis and was worshipped as 'Sarapis' in his funerary temple. Due to this confusion the temple was thenceforth called the Sarapeum.

127

Other sacred bulls

There were in addition many other sacred bulls but the three most important bulls of Egypt after Apis were Mnevis, Buchis and Onuphis.

Mnevis is the Greek rendering of Merwer, the Bull of Meroe also called Menuis. He was the bull sacred to Ra-Atum at Heliopolis. It seems that he was of a light colour, although Plutarch speaks of his black hide.

Buchis, the Greek for Bukhe, was the bull sacred to Mont at Hermonthis. According to Macrobius, the hair of his hide, which changed colour every hour, grew in the opposite direction from that of an ordinary animal. The great vaults, where the mummies of Buchis were buried, were discovered near Armant beside tombs of the cows which bore these sacred bulls.

Onuphis, the Greek rendering of Aa Nefer, 'the very good', was the bull in which the soul of Osiris was said to be incarnated, as Ra-Atum reappeared in Mnevis and Mont was re-embodied in Buchis.

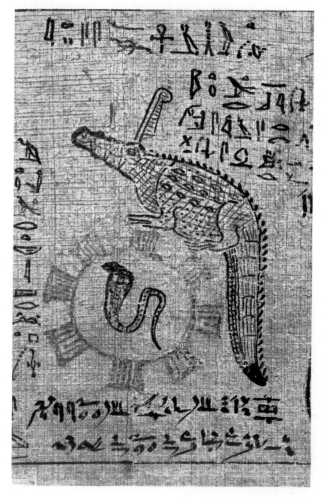

Above: *Painted coffin lid of Ankhesnefer showing the bull of Amentt (thought to be a symbol of Osiris) carrying the dead man on his back. Twenty-sixth Dynasty (664–525 B.C.). British Museum.*

Left: *Detail from a magical papyrus which was a guide for the owner on his journey through the Underworld. The crocodile was the emblem of Sebek, the deity of Ombos, and was also thought to be a deified form of the sun. British Museum.*

Right: *A temple wall-relief of Harsaphes, the ram-headed god, wearing the atef crown.*

Petesuchos

Petesuchos is the Greek rendering of an Egyptian word meaning 'he who belongs to Suchos (or Sebek)'. He was the sacred crocodile in which was incarnated the soul of Sebek, the great god of the Fayyum who had his chief sanctuary in Crocodilopolis, the capital of the province, which was called Arsinoe from the time of the second Ptolemy.

Petesuchos was venerated at Crocodilopolis, in a lake near the great temple. He was an old crocodile who wore golden rings in his ears. His devotees riveted bracelets to his forelegs.

In the Graeco-Roman period the crocodiles of Arsinoe were a great attraction for tourists. Strabo tells us how in the reign of Augustus he paid a visit to Petesuchos. 'He is fed,' Strabo writes, 'with the bread, meat and wine which strangers always bring when they come to see him. Our friend and host, who was one of the notabilities of the place and who took us everywhere, came to the lake with us, having saved from our luncheon a cake, a piece of the roast and a small flagon of honey. We met the crocodile on the shore of the lake. Priests approached him and while one of them held open his jaws another put in the cake and the meat and poured in the honey-wine. After that the animal dived into the lake and swam towards the opposite shore. Another visitor arrived, also bringing his offering. The priests ran round the lake with the food he had brought and fed it to the crocodile in the same manner.'

Sacred rams

Sacred rams were also popular in Egypt. Chief among them was Ba Neb Djedet, 'the soul of the lord of Djedet', a name which in popular speech was contracted into Banaded and in Greek rendered as Mendes. In him was incarnated the soul of Osiris, and the story which Herodotus brought back about the ram — which he wrongly calls 'the He-goat of Mendes' — confirms the veneration in which this sacred animal was held. Thoth himself, said his priests, had formerly decreed that the kings should come with offerings to the 'living ram'. Otherwise infinite misfortune would spread among men. When Banaded died there was general mourning; on the other hand immense rejoicing greeted the announcement that a new ram had been discovered, and great festivals celebrated the enthronement of this king of Egyptian animals.

Right: *The ichneumon was venerated for its hostility to the crocodile, whose eggs it destroyed.*

Far right: *The cat was sacred throughout Egypt, especially at Bubastis. Honoured also in death, the bodies were frequently embalmed, mummified and buried with all the pomp accorded to human rites. British Museum.*

The Bennu bird

The Bennu bird must also be mentioned among the sacred animals; for, though he was purely legendary, the ancients did not doubt his reality. Worshipped at Heliopolis as the soul of Osiris, he was also connected with the cult of Ra and was perhaps even a secondary form of Ra. He is identified, though not with certainty, with the phoenix who, according to Herodotus' Heliopolitan guides, resembled the eagle in shape and size, while Bennu was more like a lapwing or a heron. The phoenix, it was said, appeared in Egypt only once every five hundred years. When the phoenix was born in the depths of Arabia he flew swiftly to the temple of Heliopolis with the body of his father which, coated with myrrh, he piously buried there.

Other animals

Much more still remains to be said on the subject of the other sacred animals, veneration of which grew in proportion as foreign influence increased, for the priests recognised that divine association with animals was the most characteristically Egyptian feature of their ancient religion. In most sanctuaries an animal was fed in whom the god or goddess of the locality was supposed to be incarnate: a cat in the temple of Bast, a falcon or an ibis in the temple of Horus or Thoth. In addition, popular superstition in later times so grew that every individual of the species of animal in whose body the provincial god was incarnate was regarded as sacred by the inhabitants of that province. It was forbidden to eat them, and to kill one was a heinous crime. Since, however, different nomes venerated different animals it could happen that a certain species which was the object of a cult in one province was mercilessly hunted in the neighbouring province. This sometimes gave rise to fratricidal wars such as that which, in the first century A.D., broke out between the Cynopolitans and the Oxyrhynchites. The latter had killed and eaten

dogs to avenge themselves on the former for having eaten an oxyrhynchid, a kind of spider crab. Plutarch writes:

'In our days, the Cynopolitans having eaten a crab, the Oxyrhynchites took dogs and sacrificed them and ate their flesh like that of immolated victims. Thus arose a bloody war between the two peoples which the Romans put an end to after severely punishing both.'

Certain animals — cats, hawks, ibis — were venerated all over Egypt and to kill them was punishable by death. 'When one of these animals is concerned,' writes Diodorus, 'he who kills one, be it accidentally or maliciously, is put to death. The populace flings itself on him and cruelly maltreats him, usually before he can be tried and judged. Superstition towards these sacred animals is deeply rooted in the Egyptian's soul, and devotion to their cult is passionate. In the days when Ptolemy Auletes was not yet allied to the Romans and the people of Egypt still hastened to welcome all visitors from Italy and, for fear of the consequences, carefully avoided any occasion for complaint or rupture, a Roman killed a cat. The populace crowded to the house of the Roman who had committed this 'murder'; and neither the efforts of magistrates sent by the king to protect him nor the universal fear inspired by the might of Rome could avail to save the man's life, though what he had done was admitted to be accidental. This is not an incident which I report from hearsay, but something I saw myself during my sojourn in Egypt.'

Cats, indeed, were so venerated that when a building caught fire the Egyptians, Herodotus tells us, would neglect the fire in order to rescue these animals, whose death to them seemed more painful than any other loss they might sustain. When one of the sacred animals died it was considered to be an act of great merit to provide for its funeral; for certain animals such as the bull Apis the king himself made it his duty to take charge of the obsequies.

Pity for dead animals reached an almost unbelievable degree. Crocodile cemeteries have been discovered where the reptiles were carefully mummified and buried with their newly born and even with their eggs. Animals, birds, fish, reptiles of all kinds that were venerated by the ancient inhabitants of the Nile valley were interred by the hundreds of thousands.

**Life after death:
the spread of
the Osiris cult**

The Egyptian religion, as we have seen, was one whose creed was not laid down in a rigid formula, but was open to constant reinterpretation through cult and usage, and this in turn depended in part on external political or historical influences. As a religion embodied in the cult rather than in the doctrine, it could keep alive only through the constant search of its adepts for new interpretations. It therefore adapted itself to the needs of the times and to the needs of the particular worshipper. The search for new symbols went on constantly: each one was considered to represent one facet of the truth and did not necessarily entail rejection of previously held concepts. Equally, as the symbols changed, so shifts of emphasis could occur over the centuries as to the interpretation of the myths.

The modern reader must constantly bear in mind that the Egyptian myths, unlike the Greek or the Roman, cannot be considered as fixed stories. Their function in the Egyptian religion is to provide a notation of symbols with which to express ideas; if the ideas changed, then the myth also had to change. No myth is a better illustration of this principle than that of Osiris, which during the course of history underwent almost a complete reversal — of significance if not altogether of form.

The beginnings of the Osiris cult

From what we can guess of his origin, we suppose that Osiris was at first the fetish of a conquering clan which installed its god at Djedu, in the centre of the Delta region of Lower Egypt. This city was later named after him Per-Usire, 'the House of Osiris' (Greek, Busiris). In Djedu, Osiris took the place of the former Lord of the City, Andjeti, a god associated with fertility cults and represented in human form as a king with the royal insignia of a long crooked sceptre and a whip in his hands and with two feathers on his head. Identification of Osiris with Andjeti was facilitated by the fact that both were always represented as human beings. Osiris soon took the name Andjeti as an epithet and became known as 'Lord of Djedu'.

In the earliest times the king was credited with the power to influence or control natural phenomena, simply because of his own great power. In later periods, the king was merely considered the intermediary between the gods, particularly the sun-god, and human beings and as such their only hope of securing the benevolence of the gods of nature and the benefits which they could confer. As we have already seen, the kings were

Left: *An imposing statue of Osiris, supreme god and judge of the dead. Luxor.*

Above: *A colossus of Osiris, abandoned near an ancient granite quarry outside Aswan.*

133

ritually identified in the solar doctrines as 'sons of Ra'. In either case, the benefits which the king brought to his land were benefits of nature. As recounted in the earlier discussion of the Osiris myth, he was originally supposed to have been an actual king of Egypt, and some Egyptologists think that this may be historically true. In that case, he would naturally transfer to his deified character attributes of a fertility-god. Whether it is because of this royal derivation or whether it is because of identification with Andjeti, who

was always depicted as a living king and a god of fertility, Osiris was in fact associated with fertility cults from a very early stage. It seems, however, that as early as the period of the *Pyramid Texts* Osiris was primarily a god of the dead. It was not until a much later stage, when he had usurped some of Ra's functions, and he and his son Horus became the chief deities with which the pharaohs identified themselves, that the fertility associations were again to acquire any great importance.

Papyrus showing Osiris seated and swathed in mummy wrappings. He gave to those who passed the final ordeal his name and blessings of eternal felicity.

Right: *Stela dedicated to a protective divinity and inscribed with scenes from the judgment of the dead. British Museum.*

Osiris as king of the dead

In the earliest stages of his development in the historical period, therefore, Osiris was firmly fixed as a god of the dead. Though represented as a king, he is always shown as a dead king — a mummy bearing the royal insignia. His cult spread rapidly into Upper Egypt and he became identified with the funerary god of Abydos, Khenti-Amentiu, who was represented as a wolf. Osiris now became known as Osiris Khenti-Amentiu, 'Lord of the Westerners'. The 'West' to the Egyptians was the abode of the dead, as it was of the setting sun, and the 'Westerners' were therefore the dead.

Though the original cult-centre of Osiris was, as we have seen, at Busiris, in the Delta, it soon shifted to Abydos, in Upper Egypt, where the tomb was found of a king of the First Dynasty, Djer, whose name was misread as 'Khent'. It was believed that this was the tomb of Osiris himself. A further legend connecting Osiris with Abydos relates that Isis found her husband's head there. A local fetish of Abydos found on monuments consists of the remains of this head, set on a pole and adorned with a wig, feathers and horns. Abydos became a favoured burial ground; or in lieu of actual burial at Abydos, the Egyptians frequently had stelae erected there for the benefit of their departed.

As well as absorbing the gods Khenti-Amentiu and Andjeti, Osiris became identified with the god Seker, a necropolis god of Giza, near to Memphis.

As a king of the dead, Osiris' province as a god did not therefore at first seem to encroach in any way on the preserves of the other gods, who were seen as being concerned with creation and, through the pharaoh's identification with the cult of the sun-god, with the order of the present world. The spread of the cult of Osiris as a funerary god was not seriously opposed by the priests of Heliopolis. Ra remained the supreme god, and Osiris, Isis and Horus, their child, were incorporated in the family of Ra, the solar pantheon.

Osiris' sphere was quite clearly delimited as a minor god of another world. He did not even in the early stages have supremacy in the world of the dead, for Ra was the most important figure in the Underworld as well as in the heavens. In the form of Auf, the dead sun, he journeyed every night through the twelve provinces of the Underworld, speaking to the souls of the dead, admonishing those souls which were evil, shedding light and encouragement on the good souls of the dead. Just as there were good men and bad on earth, so there were good and bad souls in the Underworld, and evil-intentioned and well-intentioned funerary deities. Ra, or rather Auf, has to be defended against the onslaughts of the evil spirits, who often take the form of monstrous serpents, but he always succeeds in emerging into the life of a new day. Osiris, in the early stages, was, however, one of those spirits of the Underworld who might on one occasion be well-disposed and might on another be a threat to the safety of Ra.

As we have seen, the pharaoh was considered in the solar religion to be either the incarnation of Horus the Elder, son of Ra, or the physical son of Ra himself. It was natural therefore to suppose that the pharaoh, like the sun, would be resurrected after death provided the evil spirits of the Underworld were pacified. One of the essential conditions for the continued life of the soul after death was believed, from primitive times, to be the preservation of the body. From the earliest days when the Osirian legend had been incorporated into the solar religion embalmment was therefore practised. It was thought that this together with the provision of food, servants and a collection of spells (known to us as *The Book of the Dead*) to ward off any ill-intentioned spirits would assure the dead king's soul of a safe passage through the twelve provinces of the Underworld and into eternal life. The beliefs about the pharaoh thus exactly mirrored those about the sun who, as we have noted, was also represented as an embalmed body in the night-barque. The gods which formed the crew of the solar boat were enjoined in prayers to defend the soul of the dead pharaoh also.

Sennofer and his sister Merit. From the Tomb of Sennofer at Thebes.

Osiris as symbol of resurrection

The new pharaoh, being the chief priest as well as the descendant or embodiment of Horus, was naturally prominent in the ritual associated with the death of his father. This, combined with the ever-growing popularity of the Osiris cult, may help to explain how he came to be confused with the other example of filial piety in the Egyptian pantheon, namely Horus, son of Osiris. As a result of this confusion, the burial rites of the pharaohs were now associated not only with the daily rebirth of the sun, but also with the resurrection of Osiris — himself once an earthly king — as king in the after world. Just as the resurrection of Osiris was contingent on the establishment on the throne of his son Horus, so the assumption of power of the new pharaoh was the signal for and was confirmed by the passing of the old pharaoh into eternal life. It may be conjectured that this double identification would confer double assurance of life in the after world. At this stage the aspect of the Osirian myth relating to Horus most stressed may well have been that he was concerned to reclaim his kingdom from the usurper Set, rather than that he wished to avenge the murder of his father. It seems that the chief issue in the 'Great Quarrel' was whether Set or Horus should have the throne, i.e. whether the claims of seniority or of descent should have priority in matters of land tenure. At this phase in the development of Osirian beliefs it would seem that a balance has been struck. Both Osiris and Ra are invoked in the funerary rites of the pharaoh and each is deemed to have power in the land of the dead.

Perhaps the crucial circumstance which assured the further development of the Osiris cult was the collapse of the centralised government at the end of the Sixth Dynasty (2250 B.C.). In the political uncertainty which followed intellectual activity flourished and many old assumptions were questioned. The burial rites accorded to the pharaoh had already been extended to his immediate family and the aristocracy, but from this time on they were increasingly adopted by the common people. The solar ritual was obviously more suited to the king than to any of his subjects. His life was open to ritual practices and could be ordered in a semblance of the solar ritual. Besides this, as chief

The suppliant Nekhtarch. Louvre.

priest of Ra, the pharaoh had obvious connections with him; the common people were unable to approach the inner sanctuary of Ra's temples. But all men die, leaving behind grieving relatives; it was far easier for the common man to identify himself with Osiris. In addition to all this, we have shown how the cult of the sun-god was bound up with laws about the ownership and inheritance of power or property; it explained the political order of the present world. The Osiris myth, on the other hand, was one which appealed strongly to the basic human emotions. Its strength was founded in the first instance on the pathos of a good man being murdered by his evil brother but eventually attaining eternal life through the unceasing efforts of his loving wife. Osiris was a man who suffered injustice; his nature was passive. The ordinary man could identify his own destiny with that of Osiris where he was quite unable to identify it with that of the creator god.

At the same time the connection of Osiris with fertility was revived or born for the first time. Just as human beings could hope for life after death through Osiris, so through him plant and animal life were constantly renewed. It need hardly be stressed that in an agricultural land such as Egypt, where the seasons present dramatic changes and the whole population is dependent on the nature of these changes, it is only natural that the chief god should become associated with them. Such, no doubt, was originally the concept behind the solar religion, though it later acquired other, political connotations through association with the royal house. As the Osiris cult spread, so it usurped functions of the sun-cult. Equally important in the natural cycle of Egyptian agriculture was the Nile, whose floodwaters dramatically brought life to the parched land. Osiris accordingly became identified with the Nile. Just as Ra had once been considered the supreme self-generative principle, so now Osiris became the tutelary divinity of the fertile lands of the Nile valley, the god of floods and vegetation. A common practice became to fill a mummy-shaped linen case with corn seed, to water it and to let the seedlings grow through the linen. This representation was known as the 'Corn Osiris'. In the legend, Osiris' body is enclosed in

a tamarisk tree, which grows to an enormous size — a sign of the god's power to bring fertility.

It was perhaps at this stage that Set came to be considered the personification not simply of contentiousness and low cunning or, in the political interpretation, of Upper Egypt subjected to Lower Egypt, but of the desert, of storms and of barrenness. For he is now no longer the adversary of Horus, son of Ra; he has assumed the role of adversary of Horus, chief upholder of the dignity and rights of Osiris, and the murderer of Osiris himself.

It has been remarked that fertility cults are often associated by agricultural peoples with the cult of the dead. Osiris' growth as a fertility-god may therefore have reinforced his claims as funerary divinity.

The spread of the burial rites to the whole people seems, however, to have been the decisive factor in determining the further growth of the Osiris cult at the expense of the solar religion. All men, not just the king, now hoped that they would enjoy eternal life, and Osiris was the means by which they hoped to achieve it. Osiris had by now lost his character of frightening spirit of the Underworld: his example represented hope.

True to their traditions, the Egyptians did not entirely discard their former beliefs, and to some extent they still felt it necessary to pacify Osiris — as we shall see Osiris was also the judge of souls, and had to be satisfied that the dead man was sufficiently virtuous to be admitted. But the chief hope of survival in the after life was to identify completely with the passion of Osiris and to copy the exact forms of his embalmment.

Painted lid of the sarcophagus of Soter, archon of Thebes. Second century A.D. *British Museum.*

Embalmment and burial rites

From the moment of death the deceased's name was prefaced with the name 'Osiris'. The ancient Egyptian would refer to a dead man as 'Osiris X' just as we might say 'the late X'. The ritual embalmment usually took about seventy days and was a very complicated process. Its degrading aspects were certainly considered to be the dead man's way of partaking in the passion of Osiris. The dead man's body was taken away from his home to a special workshop in the form of a tent which was called 'the good house' or 'the place of purification'. First the body was washed with Nile water. Then an incision was made in the left side and the liver, lungs, stomach and intestines were removed. These organs were placed in four vessels called Canopic jars and their place in the body was taken by balls of linen. The brain, too, was removed through the nostrils and the cavity filled with linen or with mud. The purpose of the linen padding was to preserve the features intact; it was believed that if they disintegrated the personality would also disintegrate. The heart was left in the body, for it was the seat of the intelligence. The body was soaked in salt (natron) and then with various oils and resins. Amulets were placed on it, one of the most important being a scarab, placed over the heart, and, as symbol of renewed life, intended to stimulate the rebirth into eternal life. The body was then wrapped in linen

bandages and put in the coffin. All the materials used in embalmment were believed to have grown from the tears shed by the gods at the death of Osiris, and their use in the embalming rites therefore conferred on the dead man the power of these gods.

The embalmers took the roles of the gods who had helped Isis embalm Osiris. They were led by 'Anubis' and were identified with the sons of Horus and of Khentekhtay. Female mourners, usually the wife of the deceased and a female relative, but sometimes priestesses, impersonated Isis and Nephthys and, like them, kept watch over the body until burial. According to the original Osiris legend, Isis had to guard her husband's body until Horus regained the throne, for until then he would be dead; his resurrection was impossible until Horus had avenged him. The relatives of the dead man therefore had an especial duty to attend in every detail to the prescribed rites — not only for love of the deceased, but because an evil demon in the Underworld, which he might become if they neglected their duties, could do them, and especially their children, harm. The mourners therefore set off with the coffin to take it to the tomb. A great procession was formed headed by the coffin lying in a boat and drawn along on a sledge by men and oxen. At either end of the coffin knelt the two chief women mourners,

taking the roles of Isis and Nephthys and called 'kites' after the form sometimes assumed by these goddesses. Behind the coffin walked the male mourners. Then came another sledge with the Canopic jars, and finally the other women mourners, some being professional mourners, crying out their lamentations. Priests took part in the procession as they did in the actual embalmment. The procession was brought up in the rear by servants bearing the things which the deceased was supposed to need in the next world. These included food, clothes, furniture and paintings or models of his household servants and other necessities of life. It was thought that the presence of these in the tomb would ensure their provision for the dead man in the next world. This practice can be attributed to beliefs in magic powers similar to those of speech and writing, which in the form of papyri or wall-paintings were also provided to ward off evil spirits and to state the dead man's case before his divine judge.

The procession made its way towards the burial ground, which was often on the far, western bank of the Nile. They would therefore have to embark on the Nile, where they would ritually re-enact journeys actually taken by the pharaoh's funeral procession to the chief cult centres of Osiris at Busiris and at Abydos. Dancers and musicians joined the procession at the tomb. Here, the

Left: *Papyrus detail showing Nephthys and Isis, the divine mourners, with the dead man, while on the right Anubis and Horus guard the* tat, *or four-barred symbol of stability, which here has a human head wearing the crown of Upper Egypt. Bibliothèque Nationale.*

Figures of bakers found in a tomb of c. 2000 B.C.

Below: *Model of the sacred barge which carried the deceased to the other world. Prow and stern are fashioned in the form of the head of Hathor, guardian of the cemeteries of the dead. Twelfth Dynasty.*

mummy was stood upright and the ceremony of 'Opening of the Mouth' was performed. This ceremony corresponded to the occasion of Horus' visit to his father after he had finally been awarded the throne and by ousting Set had avenged his father's murder. Horus came to perform three tasks: to announce his victory to his father; to present him with the symbol of that victory, which was the eye which Set snatched out in their battle, and which has been presented to Horus in sign of victory; and to 'open his mouth'. To do this, Horus touched his father's lips with an adze which represented the Great Bear and with which, in an ancient myth, Set had opened the mouths of the gods, i.e. given them their power of command. When Horus had performed these three tasks his father was woken from his unconsciousness, and the resurrection of his soul was achieved. Similarly, in the burial rites, the ceremony of 'Opening of the Mouth' is performed in order, ritually, to open the way for the rebirth of the deceased's soul. The mummy was then placed in a coffin, usually of

Right: *The scribe Ani, as a human-headed hawk, revisits a body in the tomb. British Museum.*

Below: *The spearmen of Asyut. The capital of a province in Upper Egypt, Asyut was the centre of the worship of the jackal-headed Anubis. Objects of daily importance were buried with the dead so that they should have them in a future existence.*

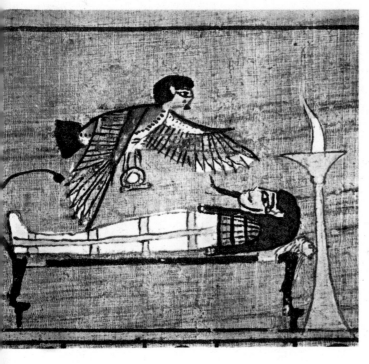

stone, or even in three or more coffins the better to withstand decay. The tumulus which surmounted the tomb was shaped rather like a house, or in the case of a king, like a palace.

Provided that the family meticulously observed the rites of embalmment, the dead man's soul would at least get as far as the Hall of Judgment in the Underworld. There he would be answerable for himself. Previously, many of the spells employed in funerary papyri were intended to disarm the gods invoked — either, seemingly, by flattery, or by vigorous assertion that the dead man had faithfully worshipped the god concerned, or again by magic spells whereby, like Isis in the legend of the serpent poisoning Ra, the dead man got the better of the god — rendering him impotent by trickery. Such practices persisted towards the other gods — though to a much lesser degree; but tricks were rarely played on Osiris, who now came to be regarded as a just and kindly king, the principle of good who through his son had triumphed over Set, the principle of evil.

Below: *Mourners at the funeral of Ani. Members of the deceased's family took a prominent part in the funerary rites. Papyrus of Ani. British Museum.*

Judgment of the dead

Horus, when he came before the tribunal of the gods in the dispute with Set, eventually was given a favourable verdict and awarded the kingdom because he was found to be 'true of voice', that is, honourable or innocent of the charges laid against him by Set. Likewise, according to some versions of the story, the dead Osiris, supported by Isis and Nephthys, was made to come forward for trial at the same hearing, and he too was found to be 'true of voice'. In order, therefore, that the dead man should be completely identified with every stage of the Osiris legend, it was imagined that his soul, too, was judged in the Underworld. It was no longer sufficient for the priests to recite magic spells or for the body to be accompanied by a papyrus containing such spells; since the cult had spread to benefit everyone, not just the divine pharaoh, it was thought that eternal life and happiness had to be earned by righteousness.

Judgment of souls may in early times have been thought of as the prerogative of Ra; but the judge of the dead was generally considered to be Osiris, 'the Good One', redeemer and judge who awaited his 'son who came from earth'. Osiris was pictured as being seated on a throne in a great Hall of Judgment called the 'Hall of the Two Truths'. The throne stood at the top of a flight of steps which represented the primeval hill on which originally Ra had been born and had begun creation, but which increasingly came to be associated with the resurrection in the after life — one example of how Osiris usurped the attributes of the sun-god. The

throne itself was enclosed within a shrine in the form of a wooden coffin decorated like the thrones of the pharaohs with *uraeus* serpents and with the hawk-headed god Seker (identified with Osiris) on the top of its lid. Osiris, sitting on the throne, was dressed in a tightly fitting robe of feathers, symbol of righteousness. He has all the insignia of royalty and of divinity: the atef crown and the royal crooked sceptre and whip and also the *uas* sceptre, carried only by the gods. His face was coloured green — a reference to his function as god of fertility. Behind him stood Isis and Nephthys and in front of him the four sons of Horus: Imset, Hapy, Duamutef and Qebehsenuf, the guardians of the Canopic jars. Anubis is also in attendance. All around the hall were forty-two judges, dressed in winding-sheets and each holding a sharp-edged sword in his hand. These judges represented the forty-two provinces of Upper and Lower Egypt and each had the task of examining some special aspect of the deceased's conscience. Some had human heads and others the heads of animals. In addition to these representatives of the provinces were the 'Great Nine' and the 'Little Nine'. The 'Great Nine' were all seated on their own thrones and consisted of Ra-Harakhte, the sun-god, sitting in his barque with, behind him, his other form, Atum, and the other gods of the Heliopolitan Ennead: Shu, Tefnut, Geb, Nut, Isis, Nephthys and Horus. Osiris does not reappear among these deities; the ninth deity is Hathor. They are attended by Hu ('Authoritative Utterance') and

Saa ('Intelligence') whom we have met before as attendants in the solar barque. The 'Little Nine' are bearded deities associated with funerary ritual.

When the deceased had, thanks to the talismans placed on his mummy and especially thanks to the passwords written on the indispensable *Book of the Dead* with which he was furnished, safely crossed the terrifying stretch of country between the land of the living and the kingdom of the dead, he was immediately ushered into the presence of his sovereign judge, either by Anubis or by Horus. After he had kissed the threshold he penetrated into the 'Hall of the Two Truths', or 'Hall of Double Justice', as it is sometimes called.

The deceased himself began the proceedings and without hesitation recited what has been called 'the negative confession'. He addressed each of his judges in turn and called him by name to prove that he knew him and had nothing to fear: that he was guilty of no evil actions or qualities. No admission of any sin was made, and the deceased affirmed that he was truly pure. This, the first part of the examination, would seem to be akin to the older practices towards the gods, where it was permissible — and possible — to deceive them. The strong affirmation that the soul of the deceased was without sin seems to have been regarded, like a magic spell, as sufficient to make it sinless. A spell has, indeed, been preserved for preventing the heart from betraying the soul in its deceitfulness before the divine judges.

The later beliefs particularly associated with the Osiris cult that it was necessary for the soul really to be virtuous are represented in the second part of the judicial hearing. The existence of these two conceptions of the significance of the judgment may be the reason for the name of the seat of judgment — Hall of the Two Truths.

The second part of the hearing was presided over by Thoth, god of wisdom and reason— who,

Left: *The weighing of souls from* The Book of the Dead. *Anubis, jackal-headed, weighs a vase representing the good actions of the dead man against the emblem of Truth. On the right Osiris is attended by Isis and Nephthys.*

Right: *The goddess Nut on the lid of a schist sarcophagus of Ankh-nes-nefer-ib-re, daughter of Psammetichus II. Twenty-sixth Dynasty. British Museum.*

145

Painted sarcophagus. Sometimes the deceased was drawn on the floor of the sarcophagus. Louvre.

a man's head; Meskhent, goddess of birth; Shai, fate, or the individual destiny of the deceased; and the nurse-goddess Renenet. These all testify before the judges as to the character of the deceased. Thoth stands by the balance with his scribe's palette, ready to inscribe the verdict. This verdict is arrived at independently of the 'negative confession' and seems to take no notice at all of the deceased's protestations. In one of the pans of the balance Anubis or Horus placed the figure of Mayet, or else her hieroglyph, an ostrich feather, symbol of truth. In the other he placed the heart of the deceased, which was considered to be the seat of consciousness and thus the instigator of man's actions. We do not know whether a sinful heart was heavier or lighter than Truth; only that if the heart was innocent it was equal in weight to Truth. Thoth verified the weight, and wrote the result on his tablets. If Truth and the heart were of equal weight the 'Great Nine' now ratified the favourable verdict, declaring that the innocence of the deceased is proved and that he shall not be thrown to Amemait, 'the Devourer' — a hybrid monster, part lion, part hippopotamus, part crocodile — who crouched near by, waiting to devour the hearts of the guilty.

The goddess Mayet now dressed the deceased in feathers, like Osiris, as a symbol of his righteousness and he was brought before Osiris by Horus, who announced the verdict to him, pleading that he should be offered bread and beer in the presence of Osiris himself and that he should live like the followers of Horus for ever. The deceased himself repeated that he had told no lies and that there was no sin in him, and Osiris declared that he might depart victorious and that he might mingle freely with the gods and the spirits of the dead.

The deceased, thus justified, would lead from then on a life of eternal happiness in the kingdom of Osiris. It is true that at a later stage it would be considered his duty to cultivate the god's domains and keep dykes and canals in good repair. But magic permitted him to avoid all disagreeable labour. For at burial he would have been furnished with *Shabtis* (or *Ushabtis*), meaning 'Answerers' — those little statuettes in stone or glazed composition which, when the dead man was called upon to perform some task, would hasten to take his place and do the job for him.

of course, had been instrumental in persuading the tribunal of the gods of the innocence of Osiris and of Horus. In the centre of the hall was a vast balance surmounted by a baboon, symbol of the god Thoth. Beside the balance stood Mayet, personification of the spirit of justice, or of world order. Other figures grouped about the balance were spirits closely connected with the life of the deceased: his soul in the shape of a falcon with

146

Later developments in the Osiris cult

Osiris must have seemed to the ancient Egyptians a much more accessible god than the solar divinities. No one but the pharaoh could claim to identify with the splendour of the cycle of the sun's death and rebirth. But Osiris was a man who, though just, suffered on earth at the hands of others. He was able to overcome the seeming dissolution through his own virtue (he was 'true of voice') and through the loving ministrations of his wife and son. He represented the possibility of rebirth and the power of revival — for human beings, but also for plant life. Though dead, he was the source of life. It is easy to see that the pharaohs would have no difficulty in identifying the cyclic patterns of their own reigns with the annual death and renewal of the natural world, for it was long believed that if the royal house prospered so would the land and its agriculture. Thus the pharaohs could perhaps claim identity with the personal death and rebirth of Osiris as of right. For the ordinary man, identification with Osiris was more a matter of hope and eventually of deserts: under the spread of the Osirian beliefs to the mass of the people, the Egyptian religion became less a collection of magic spells against the evil intentions of various deities and propitiation of the good deities, than an ethical system which laid down a code of conduct in this life on which would depend eternal salvation in the next.

Under Osirian influence the Egyptian religion became an optimistic one, which held out hope for every man. This in itself may account for the rapid growth in the importance of Osiris at the expense of Ra. Not all the solar beliefs were abandoned, but they were incorporated into the Osiris cult, just as once Osiris had been incorporated into the Heliopolitan Ennead. The sun-god retained his cult as Amon-Ra until the early fourth century B.C., but by Ptolemaic times he is no longer mentioned.

In the process of acquiring these extra functions, however, the character of Osiris himself changed. This change was partly due to absorption of features which properly belonged to the sun-god; but is was also due from Ptolemaic times onwards to confusion or coalescence with foreign gods.

The association of both Osiris and Isis with fertility cults was increasingly stressed from the New Kingdom onwards, and this encouraged their gradual penetration into the world of the living.

Mummy case of Artemidorus, a Greek settled in Egypt. Thebes. Third century B.C. British Museum.

Osiris now tended to become ruler of this world as well as of the Underworld and the hieroglyph for his name from the Twentieth Dynasty onwards was the solar disk rather than the eye.

The sacred bull Apis, a fertility god recognised by peculiar markings, had become widely venerated in the New Kingdom period, when he was considered to be a manifestation of Ptah, the creator god. As each bull died, another was

found to take his place, and the funeral rites were not unlike those of a king, who in the same way always had a natural successor who was accorded the same veneration as his predecessor. Like a king, or any other man who received the burial rites, Apis was identified with Osiris. He soon became so closely associated with him that a new hybrid god came into being, called Usar-Hapi, the Egyptian form of the two names. The Greeks living at Memphis in the Late Periods adopted this deity as Osorapis, and also worshipped Isis and Anubis. It was Osorapis whom Ptolemy I chose to be the official god of Egypt and Greece, which he hoped to unify. The name of the new god was Sarapis and he was represented in statues looking rather like Pluto with long hair and beard, seated on a throne with the triple-headed dog Cerberus at his feet. He was a very popular god and though an artificial creation, his cult rapidly spread. The full circle of his development was complete for the second time when in the third century A.D. Sarapis became a sort of sun-god.

This may be said to mark the end of the Egyptian religion in its native form. Though, as has been remarked, the priests tried to encourage animal-worship as being the most essentially Egyptian element in the religion, foreign influence could not be eradicated. As the cult of Osiris or Sarapis spread throughout the Greek world, so did that of Isis and of Horus the Child,

or Harpokrates, as he was called in Greek. Isis became the chief goddess, but in the character of a mother-goddess, and she was generally depicted suckling the child Harpokrates. It is thought by some that excessive worship of the Virgin and Child by some early Christians may owe something to the influence of this widespread cult in the Roman Empire. The cult of Isis was resisted by the early Roman emperors, for she had been the goddess of Cleopatra, but in the reign of Caligula a temple dedicated to Isis was built near Rome and under Vespasian she and Sarapis appeared on imperial coins. Caracalla had a temple of Isis built in Rome itself. Hathor, Subek and Imhotep were also worshipped under the Roman Empire, and the Egyptian deities spread to every part of it.

The Egyptian gods may have owed much of their popularity outside Egypt and their strength in the face of other deities within Egypt to the sure faith they offered of life after death. The Greek and Roman deities had become figures in stylised myths which bore comparatively little relation to the everyday concerns of their worshippers. The myths were stories told largely for entertainment and the gods depicted in them lacked mystery. The Egyptian deities, on the other hand, even during the Graeco-Roman period never lost their symbolic associations with the all-important cycles of birth and death, agelessly significant.

Left: *Mummy of a Greek boy whose head is portrayed on a wooden panel. Second century A.D. British Museum.*

A list of animals
whose heads appear
on Egyptian divinities

The following alphabetical list of those animals whose heads were borne by certain of the gods should prove useful to those interested in Egyptian mythology. Only the gods mentioned in this study are listed. We have omitted the countless genii and lesser divinities who on tomb decorations and in illustrations of funerary papyri were also represented with animal heads.

Bull:	*Osorapis. See also Apis, Mont*
Cat:	*Bast. (Sometimes, perhaps, Mut)*
Cow:	*Hathor, Isis when identified with Hathor. See also Nut.*
Crocodile:	*Sebek*
Dog-faced ape:	*Hapy, Thoth at times*
Donkey:	*Set (in later times)*
Falcon:	*Ra-Harakhte, Horus, Mont, Khons Hor, Qebehsenuf*
Frog:	*Heket*
Hippopotamus:	*Taueret*
Ibis:	*Thoth*
Jackal:	*Anubis, Duamutef*
Lion:	*Nefertum, sometimes*
Lioness:	*Sekhmet, Tefnut (sometimes Mut and Renenet)*
Ram with curved horns:	*Amon*
Ram with wary horns:	*Khnum, Hershef or Harsaphes*
Scarab:	*Khepri*
Scorpion:	*Selket*
Serpent:	*Buto. See also Mertseger and Renenet*
Uraeus:	*See Serpent*
Vulture:	*Nekhebet*
Wolf:	*Upuaut. Khenti-Amentiu*
Indeterminate animal (called Typhonian Animal):	*Set*

Index